ISBN 978-1-330-96663-1
PIBN 10127443

FB &c Ltd, Dalton House, 60 Windsor Avenue, London, SW19 2RR.
Company number 08720141. Registered in England and Wales.

For support please visit www.forgottenbooks.com

"Le philosophe, en étudiant les lois de la Nature, acquiert chaque jour la conviction que de leur violation seule naissent tous les maux dont gémit l'humanité."

"The philosopher, in studying the laws of Nature, acquires more deeply every day the conviction that from their abuse alone spring all the evils from which humanity is groaning."

Dr. Menville de Ponsan
(Histoire de la Femme; Vol. III., p. 3).

WOMAN FREE.

I.

Source of the Light that cheers this later day,
Science calm moves to spread her sovereign sway;
Research and Reason, ranged on either hand,
Proclaim her message to each waiting land;
In truths whose import stands but part revealed,
Till man befit himself those truths to wield;
Since to high Knowledge duties high belong,
As to the poet's power the task of worthy song.

II.

And man, from every stage of slow degree,
Amendment for his previous rule may see;
His keener conscience in our fuller time
Perceives the whilom careless act a crime,
Or finds some fancied fault to progress tend,—
By wiser vision traced to truer end;
Till, growing shrewder in the growing light,
We know no lack of good but our own lack of sight.

III.

Thus, sad at first, we mark each evil deed,
Of ignorance or will, bear fatal seed
Of suffering to others in its train,—
The guileless share its penalty of pain,—
And man's worst misery ofttimes is brought
By trespass he himself nor did nor thought ;
Austere the fiat, yet therefrom we learn
A purer life to frame, lest myriads mourn in turn.

IV.

Deep though the teaching that this truth reveals
Of fellowship of man with all that feels,
Remains the riddle that, though inmost ken
Of humblest creatures and of rudest men
Has sense of freedom as an instinct strong,—
Resenting injury as act of wrong,—
Man listed not this monitor's still voice,
But gave his wanton wish the guilty force of choice.

V.

Dark looms the record of his earlier years,—
A troubled tale of infamy and tears ;
For, of the ill by man primeval wrought,
Shows forth predominant with anguish fraught,
And long disaster to the ensuant race,
The direful course of degradation base,
Where freedom, justice, right,—at one fell blow,—
In woman's life of slave were outraged and laid low.

VI.

The inklings gleaned of prehistoric hour
Speak woman thrall to man's unbridled power ;
Than brute more gifted, he, with heinous skill,
Subdued her being to his sensual will ;
Binding her fast with ties of cunning weight,
By mother's burden forced to slavish fate ;
Thus woman was, and such her man-made doom,
Ere yet the dawn of love illumed the soulless gloom.

VII.

Ere Evolution, in unhasting speed,
Trained man's regard to larger life and need·
By Art his feelings waked to functions higher,
Disclosed within his clay the veins of fire,
Taught him his pleasures of the flesh to find
But presage of the mightier joys of mind;
Evoked the soul from fume of mortal dust,
The vestal flame of love from lower flush of lust.

VIII.

The eye that once could note but food or foe
Grew wise to watch the landscape's varied glow;
To gaze beyond our earthly temporal bars,
And track the orbit of the wandering stars:
The voice erst roused by hunger or by rage
Now tells the nobler passions of the age,
Till with love's language is uplifted love
To high and selfless thought all sensuous aim above.

IX.

But not at once such life and love to know,
For progress strives through many an ebb and flow;
Man's kindling sense, though stirred by call of Art,
Still missed the motive of her deepest heart;
'Twas in her gracious embassy to give
A fairer faith and fate to all that live,
Neglecting none,—yet man, 'twixt lust and pride,
Due portion in the boon to woman still denied.

X.

Æons of wrong ere history was born,
With added ages passed in slight and scorn,
Maintained the chains of primal womanhood,
And clogged in turn man's power of greater good;
Egypt or Greece in vain sought heavenly light
While woman's soul was held from equal flight,—
Her path confined by man to sordid end,
As subjugated wife, or hireling transient friend.

XI.

Marriage—which might have been a mateship sweet,
Where equal souls in hallowed converse meet,
Each aiding each the higher truths to find,
And raising body to the plane of mind,—
Man's baser will restrained to lower grade,
And woman's share a brainless bondage made;
Her only hope of thought or learning wide,
Some freer lot to seek than yoke forlorn of bride.

XII.

Yet, as hetaira,—comrade, chambermate,—
(The ambiguous word bespoke her dubious state),
She, craving mental food, might but be guest
By paying with her body for the quest;
Conceding that, might lead a learned life,—
A licence vetoed to the legal wife,—
Might win great wealth, or build a lasting fame,
Not due to her the guilt that left the tinge of shame.

XIII.

What guilt was there, apportion it aright
To him who fixed the gages of the fight;
Blame man, who, reckless of the woman's fate,
In greed for meaner pleasure lost the great;
Blame him, the vaunted sage, who knew her mind
Peer to his own in skill and wit refined,
Yet left the after-ages to bemoan
The waste of woman worth that dawned and died unknown.

XIV.

And deep the shame on man's insensate heart
For later woman doomed to hideous part;
Poor lostling, bowed with worse than brutal woes,—
To her not even dealt the brute's repose;
Her sweetness sullied, and her frame disgraced,
Soul scarce might light her temple fair defaced,—
Its chastest sanctities coerced to give
For painful bread to eat, for piteous chance to live.

XV.

While such her fate in lands of cultured creed,
Judge woman's griefs with man of barbarous breed;
Slave to his lust, and tiller of his soil,
Crippled and crushed by cruelty and toil;
Yet still her heart a gentle mien essayed
By deeper passion, holier impulse, swayed,
Care for her wretched offspring rarely swerved
And mother-love alone the infant oft preserved.

XVI.

Thus woman's life, in low or high estate,
Man fettered with a more than natural weight
Of sexual function,—disproportioned theme
And single basis in his female scheme;
He strove to quench her flash of quicker fire,
That crossed his lordship or his low desire;
Her one permitted end to serve his race,
Her individual soul forbidden breathing place.

XVII.

Scarce other seemed that soul than sentient tomb
Of human energy debarred to bloom;
Her spirit, pining in its durance drear,
Leaves legacy of many a burning tear
For aspirations crushed, and aims denied,
And instincts thwarted by man's purblind pride;
Her every wish made subject to the nod
Of him whose mad conceit proclaimed himself her God.

XVIII.

So stood at halt, through years of sterile change,
His narrowed brain and her restricted range;
And man intelligent and woman free,
Was union which the world had yet to see;
For time to come reserved the golden sight
Of glorious harvest from the natural right,
To her as amply as to him assigned
To compass power unknown in body and in mind.

XIX.

Happy the epoch destinied to show
What force of good from that free fate shall flow ;
The artificial limits to efface
Of laws and forms that womanhood debase ;
Even our own imperfect hour may prove
The ecstasy of earnest souls that move
In dual union of unselfish strife
To reach by mutual love to true and equal life.

XX.

Yet slow, so slowly, gleams the gathering light,
And lingers still the hovering shade of night ;
Though part undone the wrong that we confess,
Repentance cannot instant bring redress ;
Nor woman, tortured by her thraldom long,
At once stand forth emancipate and strong ;
Her pain persistent, though she calm suppress
Her rancour for the past, with sweet forgivingness.

XXI.

For carnal servitude left cruel stain,
And galls that fester from the fleshly chain ;
Unhealed the scars of man's distempered greed,
The wounds of blind injustice still they bleed ;
Recurrent suffering lets her not forget
The aimless payments of a dismal debt,—
Survival from dim age of man's abuse
Of functions immature, profaned by savage use.

XXII.

Her girlhood's helpless years through cycles long
Had been a martyrdom of sexual wrong,
For little strength or choice might child oppose
To shield herself from force of sensual foes ;
Impending motherhood might win no rest
Or refuge sacred from the satyr quest ;
Unripe maternity, untimely birth,
The woman's constant dole in those dark days of earth.

XXIII.

Action repeated tends to rhythmic course,
And thus the mischief, due at first to force,
Brought cumulative sequence to the race,
Till habit bred hereditary trace;
On woman falls that heritage of woe,
And e'en the virgin feels its dastard blow,—
For, long ere fit to wield maternal cares,
Abnormal fruits of birth her guiltless body bears.

XXIV.

Misread by man, this sign of his misdeed
Was held as symptom of her nubile need,
And on through history's length her tender age
Has still been victim to his adult rage;
He, by his text, with irony serene,
Banned her resultant "manner" as "unclean";
The censure base upon himself recoils,
Yet leaves the woman wan and cumbered in his toils.

XXV.

Vicarious punishment for manhood's crime
Takes grievous toll of all her active prime ;
The hap, in educated woman's fate,
Is instinct with antipathy and hate
Reason confirming tells, no honest claim
Could ever cause such gust of inward shame,
Nor act of normal wont might man blaspheme
To make of Nature's need a vile opprobrious theme.

XXVI.

Thoughts like to these are breathings of the truth
To whoso ponders deep the tale of ruth ;
The futile mannish pleas that would explain
The purport of her periodic pain,
All bear unconscious witness to the wrong
In blindness born, in error fostered long,—
The spurious function growing with the years,
Till almost natural use the morbid mode appears.

XXVII.

Grievous the hurt to woman, which to right
Is instant duty of our stronger sight ;
From off her wearv shoulders, bruised and worn,
To lift the cross in longtime misery borne ;
Until, reintegrate in frame and mind,
A speedy restitution she shall find,
From every trammel of man's mastery freed,
Nor held by his behest from fullest life and deed.

XXVIII.

And soon may pass her suffering, for the ill
By man begot lies subject to our skill ;
All human malady may be allayed
With human forethought, human action's aid ;
Ours then the fault, since, given in our hand
Is power the evil hazard to command ·
For Nature, kindly wise our woes to shape,
In very pang of pain both prompts and points escape.

XXIX.

So woman shall her own redemption gain,
Instructed by the sting of bootless pain;
With Nature ever helpful to retrieve
The injury we heedlessly achieve,
From seed of act, by recent woman sown,
Already guerdon rich in hope is shown;—
Such faculty her new-found presence decks,
The sage physician, she, and saviour of her sex.

XXX.

With purer phase of life proves woman less
The burden of the wasting weariness;
And thus, in rank refined or rude have grown
Maidens in whom the weakness was not known;
Hale woman and true mother have they been,
Yet never have the noisome habit seen·
Not to neglectful man to greatly care
How such immunity all womanhood might share.

XXXI.

Her intellect alert the harm shall heal,
And ways of wholesomeness and strength reveal;
The saving truth she wins with studious thought
More swiftly to her daughter shall be taught,—
How body still is supple unto mind,
By dint of soul is fleshly form inclined,
And woman's will shall work of man atone,
The deed his darkness wrought be by her light undone.

XXXII.

No longer drilled deformity to nurse,
And woo, when slow to appear, the absent curse,
Her counter-effort, helped by Nature's grace,
Shall quell the "custom's" last abhorrent trace;
Its morbid usurpation shall refute,—
Not more to woman natural than to brute;—
A needless noyance with a baseless claim,
The lingering mark of man's unthinking guilt and shame.

XXXIII.

Her body, saved from enervating drain,
Shall lend a newer vigour to the brain;
Wide shall she roam in realms of untold thought,
Which ages since her shackled instinct sought;
For oft her prison had the yearnings heard,
In murmurings scarce rendered into word;—
Promptings which man suspicious strove to choke,
Lest that her soul should rise and break his time-worn yoke.

XXXIV.

For autocrats of old, with treacherous guile,
Had bribed the villain's soul by sensual wile;
To meanest man a lower drudge assigned,—
With gift of female thrall cajoled the hind;
The stolid churl his servitude forgave
Whilst he in turn was master to a slave;
Through every rank the sexual serfdom ran,
And woman's life was bound in vassalage to man.

XXXV.

Then, fearing that the slave herself might guess
The knavery of her forced enchainedness,
A subtle fiction mannish brain designed
To dominate her conscience and her mind,—
Inhuman dogmas did his genius frame,
Investing them with sanctimonious name
Of "woman's duty"; and the fetish base
E'en to this reasoned day uplifts its impious face.

XXXVI.

By cant condoned, man fashioned woman's "sphere,"
And mapped out "natural" bounds to her career;
His sapience—should she dare any deed
In contravention of his code—decreed
On soul or body penalties condign,
In part dubbed civil law, and part divine·
Misguided man,—confused in self-deceit
His unisexual wit and pious pretext meet.

XXXVII.

Obeisance yet his caste of sex demands ;—
In legislative script the verbiage stands
How lowest boor is lordly "baron" styled,
And highest bride as common "feme" reviled ,
The tardier fear that grants the clown a share
In his own governance, denies it her ;
And British matrons are, by man-made rules,
In solemn statute ranked with infants, felons, fools.

XXXVIII.

The crass injustice early man displayed,
His own crude infancy of brain betrayed ;
His riper judgment scorns the childish use,
And cries to all his bygone freaks a truce ;
Enactments that long blemished legal page
Shall fade as figments of a foolish age,
Till saner years have every bond erased
Which selfish law of man on life of woman placed.

XXXIX.

Till like with him in human right she stands,
Her will an equal power of rule commands;
Her voice, in council and in senate heard,
To stern debate brings harmonising word;
In mutual stress each sex the other cheers,
Since one are made their hopes and one their fears;
"Self-reverent each, and reverencing each,"—
The theme that truer man and freer woman teach.

XL.

For but a slave himself must ever be,
Till she to shape her own career be free;—
Free from all uninvited touch of man,
Free mistress of her person's sacred plan;
Free human soul; the brood that she shall bear,
The first—the truly free, to breathe our air;
From woman slave can come but menial race,
The mother free confers her freedom and her grace.

XLI.

By her the progress of our future kind,
Their stalwart body and their spacious mind;
For, folded in her form each human mite
Has its first home, its sustenance and light;
Hers the live warmth that fans its spirit flame,
Her generous sap supplies its fleshly frame,
And e'en the juice,—the fullborn infant's food,
Is yet a blanched form of woman's living blood.

XLII.

Strange wisdom by her unkenned craft is taught
While yet the embryo in her womb is wrought;
For, long ere entering on our tumult rife,
It learns from her the needful art of life;
Unconscious teacher, she, yet all she knows
Of dark experience to her infant flows,
And brands him, ere he rest upon her knee,
Offshoot of slavish race, not scion of the free.

XLIII.

To either sex the bondage and the pain,
They seek to live a freeman's life in vain;
For man or woman can but act the part,
When 'tis not freeborn blood that fills the heart
Strive as he may, the modern man, at best,
Is tyrant, differing somewhat from the rest;
Nor woman thraldom-bred can surely know
Where lies her richest gift, or how its wealth to show.

XLIV.

Thus learn we that in woman rendered free
Is raised the rank of all humanity;
The despot is the fullfruit of the slave;—
To form the freeman, equable and brave,
Habit of freedom must spontaneous come
As life itself, and from the selfsame womb;
Life, liberty, and love,—lien undefiled,—
The freeborn mother's heirloom to her freeborn child.

XLV.

So shall her noble issue, maid or boy,
With equal freedom equal fate enjoy ;
Together reared in purity and truth,
Through plastic childhood and retentive youth ;
Their mutual sports of sinew and of brain
In strength alike the sturdy comrades train ;
Of differing sex no thought inept intrudes,
Their purpose calmly sure all errant aim excludes.

XLVI.

For soul, not sex, shall to each life assign
What destiny to fill, or what decline ;
Through years mature impartial range shall reach,
And wider wisdom, juster ethics, teach ;
Conformed to claims of intellect and need,
The tempered numbers of their highborn breed ;
Not overworn with childward pain and care,
The mother—and the race—robuster health shall share.

XLVII.

Nor blankly epicene, as scoffers say,
The necessary sequence of that day;
For not by vapid imitation low,
Or aping falser sex shall truer grow;
Nor modish mind may fathom Nature's range,
Or fix the fleeting scope of human change;
Can singer blind the rainbow's tints compare?—
The brain enslaved from birth the freeman's powers declare?

XLVIII.

Work we in faith, secure that precious seed
Shall bear due fruit for man's extremest need;
Not greatly timorous, as those fruits we see,
What changed existence from such food may be;
For well we wot shall come forth worthy soul,
Or male or female, with impartial dole
Of all that life can grant of good or great,—
Happy what each may bring to help the common fate.

XLIX.

By mutual aid perfecting complex man,
Their twofold vision human life may scan
From differing standpoints, grasping from the two
A clearer concept and a bolder view ·
And thus diverse humanity shall learn
A wisdom which not single sex might earn ;
Each on the problem casting needful light,
Not fully known of one without the other's sight.

L.

How should he write what she alone may tell ?—
The movements of her psychic ebb and swell ;
The latent springs of life that in her gush,
When motherhood's first throb awakes her flush,
And swift the signal flashes to her soul,
Of future being claiming her control ;
Seeking from her its mind and body's food ;
Drawing, to make its own, her evil and her good.

LI.

Within herself the drama's scene is laid,
The Birth and Growth of Soul the mystery played ;
She, in her part, is but an agent mute,
Her brain untutored, nor her tact acute,
Her nerve-strung body slow as senseless soil
To watch the working of the seedling's toil;
In vain before her inmost vision spread
The hidden streams from whence the vital founts are fed.

LII.

The mother's blindness was blind man's decree,
And to himself reverts the misery ;
Through hapless years his ordinance has run,
And harsh reward of ignorance has won ;
His pride of maledom, dull to recognise
The deeper depth accessive to her eyes,
Forbade to teach her brain to understand
The facts that, deftly sought, lay ready to her hand.

LIII.

Less wisely he, his curious search to serve,
In helpless creature teased the quivering nerve,
And strove to probe the covert ways of life
By living butchery with learned knife,
And cruel anodyne that chained the will,
Yet left the shuddering victim conscious still·
But Nature shrinks from foul and fierce attack,
Nor yields her holiest truths on such a murderer's rack.

LIV.

True science finds its own by kindlier quest,
Nor lowers itself to torture's loathsome test;
Multiplies not the sentient being's pain,
But makes a keener lens of man's own brain;
Seeks not by outrage dire a soul to grasp,
Or dimly trace its agonising gasp;
But surer learns what fire that soul may move,
Not wrung with deathly pang, but thrilled by breath of love.

LV.

To touch of love alone will Nature pour
The choicest treasures of her occult store;
Into the ear of love alone repeat
The secret of the song our pulses beat;
To eye of love alone, with joyance bright,
Shows she her form suffused in living light;
To heart that loves her, Nature gives to know
How from Love's might alone all thoughts of Wisdom grow.

LVI.

So opes a vaster knowledge to the view,
Love points the way and woman holds the clue;
Nature on her the trustful office laid,
And arbiter of human fortune made;
With woman honoured, rises man to height,
With her degraded, sinks again in night;
Yet still the wayward race has sluggish been
To learn the fealty due to Earth's advancing queen.

LVII.

For long, in jealousy for corporal power,
Had man contemned his sister's worthier dower;
What time his ruder feelings held the sway,
With little hope or hint of truer way;
Till on a wistful world has dawned benign
The prescience of a potency divine
Sleeping, unrecked of, deep in woman's heart,
Waiting some kiss superne, into full life to start.

LVIII.

Woman's own soul must seek and find that fay,
And wake it into light of quickening day;
Man's counsel helpful in that track shall be
For all his learning rich return and fee;
His philosophic and chirurgic lore,
To her imparted, swell her innate store;
Till, clothed with majesty of mind she stand,
Regent of Nature's will, in heart, and head, and hand.

LIX.

Each sequent life shall feel her finer care,
Each heir of life a wealthier bounty share;
Those lives allied in equal union chaste
A sweeter purpose, purer rapture, taste;
Both parents vindicate the duteous name,
The troth and kinship of their linked claim;
The only rivalry that moves their mind,
How for their lineage fair still larger fate to find.

LX.

Their task ineffable yields wondrous gain,
Their energies celestial force attain;
Their intermingled souls, with passion dight,
In aspiration soar past earthly height;
Nor fades their prospect into void again,—
Woman has gift the vision to retain,
And mould their dreams of love, with conscious skill,
To human living types supreme of form and will.

LXI.

The psychic and the physical at one
In fervid vigour through their frame shall run;
Their science leaps the bounds of straiter space,
Whose crude dimensions curbed their growing grace;
Whose inefficiencies allowed not verge
For rich research their lofty souls would urge;
To them the keys of life and love are given,—
The love that lifts the life from rank of earth to heaven.

LXII.

And "winged words on which the soul would pierce
Into the height of love's rare Universe"
Shall native flow from them as mother tongue
In softest strain to listening infant sung;
Till, the sad memories of unmeant wrong
Solving in music of conciliant song,
Man's destiny with woman's blended be
In one sublime progression,—full, and strong, and free.

LXIII.

L'Envoi.

The bard of yore, the stately Florentine,—
The seer of the dream men named Divine,—
Through whose grave tones one strenuous passion rolled,
While to slow ears the voice fell stern or cold,—
In his last verse proclaimed his crowning faith,
By words whose echoes pass the bar of death ;—
As breathed his soul with Beatrice afar—
"The love that moves the sun and every circling star."

NOTES, &c.

WOMAN FREE.

NOTES, &c.

I.

2.—" *Science calm moves* .

"Science is properly more scrupulous than dogma. Dogma gives a charter to mistake, but the very breath of science is a contest with mistake, and must keep the conscience alive."—George Eliot (" Middlemarch," Chap. LXXIII.)

3.—" *Research and reason*

As indicated by Professor Oliver T. Lodge, "It is but a platitude to say that our clear and conscious aim should always be truth, and that no lower or meaner standard should ever be allowed to obtrude itself before us. Our ancestors fought hard and suffered much for the privilege of free and open inquiry, for the right of conducting investigation untrammelled by prejudice and foregone conclusions, and they were ready to examine into any phenomenon which presented itself. . Fear of avowing interest or of examining into unorthodox facts is, I venture to say, not in accordance with the highest traditions of the scientific attitude."—(Address as President of the Mathematical and Physical Section of the British Association, 1891.)

D 2

See also the words of Richard Jefferies :—"Research proceeds upon the same old lines and runs in the ancient grooves. . . . But there should be no limit placed on the mind. Most injurious of all is the continuous circling on the same path, and it is from this that I wish to free my mind."—("The Story of My Heart," Chap. X.)

5.— . . . *part revealed.*"

"We are still the early settlers in a beautiful world, whose capabilities, imperfectly known as yet, wait until higher developments of man can understand them fully, and apply the result to the general good."—Professor T. Rupert Jones (Address as President of the Geological Section of the British Association, 1891).

II.

3.— . . . *keener conscience*

"C'est l'incarnation de l'idée qui se dresse tout à coup en face des vieilles traditions obstinées et insuffisantes et elle vient . . poser sa revendication personelle et nécessaire contre les lois jadis excellentes, mais qui, les mœurs s'étant modifiées, apparaissent subitement comme des injustices et des barbaries."—A. Dumas fils ("Les Femmes qui Tuent et les Femmes qui Votent," p. 25).

IV.

7.—" . . . *monitor's still voice.*"—*Conf.* Wordsworth ;

"Taught both by what she" (Nature) "shows, and
what conceals,

Never to blend our pleasure or our pride
With sorrow of the meanest thing that feels."
("Hart-Leap Well.")

VI.

1.— . . . *prehistoric hour.*"

"The preface of general history must be compiled from the materials presented by barbarism. Happily, if we may say so, these materials are abundant. So unequally has the species been developed, that almost every conceivable phase of progress may be studied, as somewhere observed and recorded. And thus the philosopher, fenced from mistake as to the order of development, by the inter-connection of the stages and their shadings into one another by gentle gradations, may draw a clear and decided outline of the course of human progress in times long antecedent to those to which even philology can make reference."—M'Lennan ("Primitive Marriage," p. 9).

Id. "I will confine myself to these examples, gleaned from all parts, and which it would be easy to multiply. They amply suffice to establish that, in primitive societies, woman, being held in very low esteem, is absolutely reduced to the level of chattels and of domestic animals; that she represents a booty like any other; that her master can use and abuse her without fear. But in these bestial practices there is nothing which approaches even distantly to marriage, and we are not in the least warranted to call these brutal rapes marriages."—Letourneau ("Evolution of Marriage," Chap. VI.).

2.—"*woman thrall* . . ."

"Woman was the first human being that tasted bondage. Woman was a slave before the slave existed."—August Bebel ("Woman," Chap. I.).

Id. . "From the very earliest twilight of human society, every woman (owing to the value attached to her by man, combined with her inferiority in muscular strength) was found in a state of bondage to some man."—J. S. Mill ("The Subjection of Woman," Chap. I.).

Id. "In every country, and in every time, woman, organically weaker than man, has been more or less enslaved by him."—Letourneau ("The Evolution of Marriage," Chap. XI.).

Id. "It raised up the humble and fallen, gave spirit and strength to the poor,
And is freeing from slavery Woman, the slave of all ages gone by."
—C. G. Leland ("The Return of the Gods").

3.—" . . . *heinous skill.*"

"It is pitiful to reflect that man's vaunted superiority over the brute, the greater activity of his brain, and the subtler cunning of his hand, have for so long lent themselves to the oppression that has resulted in such pernicious consequences, and in the still existent slavery, social and physical, of the female of his own species."—Ben Elmy ("Studies in Materialism," Chap. III.).

8.—" . . . *soulless gloom.*"

Compare the following picture of the somewhat parallel condition of a lower race at the present time:—

"Natives may well call the monkey sire Maharaja, for he is the very type and incarnation of savage and sensual despotism. They are right, too, in making their Hanuman red, for the old male's face is of the dusky red you see in some elderly, overfed human faces. Like human Maharajas, they have their tragedies and mayhap their romances. One morning there came a monkey chieftain, weak and limping, having evidently been worsted in a severe fight with another of his own kind. One hand hung powerless, his face and eyes bore terrible traces of battle, and he hirpled slowly along with a pathetic air of suffering, supporting himself on the shoulder of a female, a wife, the only member of his clan who had remained faithful to him after his defeat. We threw them bread and raisins, and the wounded warrior carefully stowed the greater part away in his cheek pouch. The faithful wife, seeing her opportunity, sprang on him, holding fast his one sound hand, and, opening his mouth, she deftly scooped out the store of raisins. Then she sat and ate them very calmly at a safe distance, while he mowed and chattered in impotent rage. He knew that without her help he could not reach home, and was fain to wait with what patience he might till the raisins were finished. It was a sad sight, but, like more sad sights, touched with the light of comedy. This was probably her first chance of disobedience or of self-assertion in her whole life, and I am afraid she thoroughly enjoyed it. Then she led him away."—J. Lockwood Kipling ("Beast and Man in India").

VII.

1.— . . . *Evolution*

"We now know that Nature, as an anthropomorphic being, does not exist; that the great forces called natural are unconscious; that their blind action results, however, in the world of life, in a choice, a selection, a progressive evolution, or, to sum up, in the survival of the individuals best adapted to the conditions of their existence."—Letourneau ("The Evolution of Marriage," Chap. I., Part II.).

Id. . . "Robert Chambers's common-sense view of evolution as a process of continued growing."—Professor Patrick Geddes and J. Arthur Thomson ("The Evolution of Sex," p. 302).

3.—"*By Art*

"Other implements of Palæolithic age are formed of bone and horn. Among these are harpoon-heads, barbed on one or both sides, awls, pins, and needles with well-formed eyes. But by far the most noteworthy objects of this class are the fragments of bone, horn, ivory, and stone, which exhibit outlined and even shaded sketches of various animals. These engravings have been made with a sharp-pointed implement, and are often wonderfully characteristic representations of the creatures they pourtray. The figures are sometimes single, in other cases they are drawn in groups. We find representations of a fish, a seal, an ibex, the red-deer, the great Irish elk or deer, the bison, the horse, the cave-bear, the reindeer, and the mammoth or woolly elephant. Besides engravings, we meet also with sculptures. . . . It is impossible to say to what use all these objects were put. Some of them may have been handles for knives, while others are mere fragments, and only vague guesses can be made as to the nature of the original implements. It is highly probable, however, that many of these works of art may have been designed simply as such, for the pleasure and amusement of the draughtsman and his fellows."—James Geikie ("Prehistoric Europe," Chap. II.).

Id. The culture or appreciation of Art is of

itself evidence of a higher nature in man; "a soul, a psyche, a something which aspires," as Richard Jefferies calls it. For though the professional pursuit of Art may be occasionally not unmingled with mercenary motives, or with the pourtrayal of incentives to lower desire, yet the ultimate appeal of every truly beautiful picture or object of Art is, at any rate, not to man's mercenary or meaner nature. As Jefferies again says, "The ascetics are the only persons who are impure. The soul is the higher even by gazing on beauty."—("The Story of My Heart," Chap. VII.)

7.—" . . . *the soul* . . ."

"The mind of man is infinite. Beyond this, man has a soul. I do not use this word in the common sense which circumstances have given to it. I use it as the only term to express that inner consciousness which aspires."—Richard Jefferies ("The Story of My Heart," Chap. IX.).

8.—" . . . *from lower flush of lust.*"

"The fact to be insisted upon is this, that the vague sexual attraction of the lowest organisms has been evolved into a definite reproductive impulse, into a desire often predominating over even that of self-preservation; that this, again, enhanced by more and more subtle additions, passes by a gentle gradient into the love of the highest animals, and of the average human individual."—Geddes and Thomson ("Evolution of Sex," p. 267).

VIII.

5, 6.—"*The voice erst roused by hunger or by rage,*
Now tells the nobler passions of the age."

"The impassioned orator, bard, or musician, when, with his varied tones and cadences, he excites the strongest emotions in his hearers, little suspects that he uses the same means by which, at an extremely remote period, his half-human ancestors aroused each other's ardent passions during their mutual courtship and rivalry."—Darwin ("The Descent of Man," Chap. XIX.).

7.—" . . . *with love's language is uplifted love.*"

Language is thought, we are told; so also is love. And thus the reciprocal and cumulative action of love, thought, and language stands a corollary to Max Müller's words:—"Language and thought are inseparable. Words without thought are dead sounds; thoughts without words are nothing. To think is to speak low; to speak is to think aloud. The word is the thought incarnate."—("Science of Language," Lect. IX.)

Id. "Even the rude Australian girl (aborigine) sings in a strain of romantic affliction:

'I shall never see my darling again.'"

—Westermarck ("History of Human Marriage," p. 503).

Id. . . "And again, another benefit accrues to the race from marriages of affection. Do not your ancient epics which sing of love sing also of noble deeds and acts of heroism on the part both of men and women, actuated by a pure affection for each other? Alike in your dramas and in those of Shakespeare, and of all great writers, love is the great motive power which impels to deeds of prowess, the spring of noble actions, of unselfish devotion, of words and thoughts which have enriched all later generations, the one sentiment which elevates marriage amongst mankind to something infinitely higher and purer than the gratification of a mere animal instinct."—Dr. Edith Pechey Phipson (Address to the Hindoos of Bombay on Child Marriage, 1891, p. 14).

8.— . . . *selfless thought.*"

"Love took up the harp of life, and smote on all the
chords with might;
Smote the chord of Self that, trembling, pass'd in
music out of sight."
—Tennyson ("Locksley Hall").

IX.

7.— . . . *Neglecting none*

"We are entering into an order of things in which justice will be the primary virtue, grounded on equal, but also on sympathetic association; having its roots no longer in the instinct of equals for self-protection, but in a cultivated sympathy between them; and no one being now left out, but an equal measure being extended to all."—J. S. Mill ("The Subjection of Women," p. 80).

X.

4.—" . . . *clogged* *man's power*

"He has reaped the usual reward of selfishness, the gratification of immediate low desires has frustrated the future attainment of higher aspirations."—Mrs. Pechey Phipson, M.D. (Address to Hindoos).

5, 6.—"*Egypt or Greece in vain sought heavenly light,*
While woman's soul was held from equal flight."

In Egypt "the art (of literature) was practised only by the priests, as the painted history plainly declares. No female is depicted in the act of reading. . . . The Greek world was composed of municipal aristocracies, societies of gentlemen living in towns, with their farms in the neighbourhood, and having all their work done for them by slaves. They themselves had nothing to do but to cultivate their bodies by exercise in the gymnasium, and their minds by conversation in the market-place. They lived out of doors, whilst their wives remained shut up at home. In Greece a lady could only enter society by adopting a mode of life which in England usually facilitates her exit."—Winwood Reade ("The Martyrdom of Man," pp. 35, 71).

8.—" . *subjugated wife*

At Athens "the free citizen women lived in strict and almost Oriental recluseness, as well after being married as when single. Everything which concerned their lives, their happiness, or their rights, was determined or managed for them by their male relatives; and they seem to have been destitute of all mental culture and accomplishments."—Grote ("History of Greece," Vol. VI., p. 133).

XI.

1.—"*Marriage which might have been a mateship sweet.*"

"In vain Plato urged that young men and women should

be more frequently permitted to meet one another, so that there should be less enmity and indifference in the married life." ("Nomoi," Book VI.)—Westermarck ("History of Human Marriage," p. 361).

2.— . . . *equal souls*

"The feeling which makes husband and wife true companions for better and worse, can grow up only in societies where the altruistic sentiments of man are strong enough to make him recognise woman as his equal, and where she is not shut up as an exotic plant in a greenhouse, but is allowed to associate freely with men. In this direction European civilisation has been advancing for centuries."—Westermarck (*loc. cit.*). (See also Note XIX., 6.)

7, 8.—"*Her only hope of thought or learning wide,*
Some freer lot to seek than yoke forlorn of bride."

In Greece "the modest women were confined to their own apartments, and were visited only by their husbands and nearest relations. . . The courtesans of Athens, by living in public, and conversing freely with all ranks of people, upon all manner of subjects, acquired, by degrees, a knowledge of history, of philosophy, of policy, and a taste in the whole circle of the arts. Their ideas were more extensive and various, and their conversation was more sprightly and entertaining than anything that was to be found among the virtuous part of the sex. Hence their houses became the schools of elegance; that of Aspasia was the resort of Socrates and Pericles, and, as Greece was governed by eloquent men, over whom the courtesans had an influence, the latter also influenced public affairs." — Alexander Walker ("Woman, as to Mind," &c., p. 334).

XII.

3.— . . . *craving mental food*

That the quest of knowledge and intellectual power was literally the incentive to many a woman who accepted the life of *hetaira* is indisputable. Westermarck says:—" It seems to me much more reasonable to suppose that if, in Athens and India, courtesans were respected and sought after by the principal men, it was because they were the only educated women."—("History of Marriage," p. 81.)

And Letourneau remarks:— "Religious prostitution, which was widely spread in Greek antiquity, has been also found in India, where every temple of renown had its bayadères, the only women in India to whom, until quite recently, any instruction was given."—("Evolution of Marriage," Chap. III.)

5, 6.—" *Conceding that, might lead a learned life—*
A license vetoed to the legal wife."

" *Hetàirai*, famous at once for their beauty and intellect such as Phryne, Laïs of Corinth, Gnathæna, and Aspasia, were objects of universal admiration among the most distinguished Greeks. They were admitted to their assemblies and banquets, while the 'honest' women of Greece were, without exception, confined to the house. A considerable number of women preferred the greater freedom which they enjoyed as *Hetairai* to marriage, and carried on the trade of prostitution as a means of livelihood. In unrestrained intercourse with men, the more intelligent of the *Hetairai*, who were doubtless often of good birth, acquired a far greater degree of versatility and culture than that possessed by the majority of married women, living in a state of enforced ignorance and bondage. This invested the *Hetairai* with a greater charm for the men, in addition to the arts which they employed in the special exercise of their profession. This explains the fact that many of them enjoyed the esteem of some of the most distinguished and eminent men of Greece, to whom they stood in a relationship of influential intimacy, a position held by no legitimate wife. The names of these *Hetairai* are famous to the present day, while one enquires in vain after the names of the legitimate wives."—August Bebel ("Woman," Chap. I.).

7.—" . . . *wealth, or* . . . *fame.*"

E.g., Phryne, who offered to rebuild the wall of Thebes; and Laïs, commemorated in the adage, "*Non cuivis hominum contingit adire Corinthum.*" And as to even modern "fame," a writer so merciless concerning her own sex as Mrs. Lynn Linton can yet say, "Agnes Sorel, like Aspasia, was one of the rare instances in history where failure in chastity did not include moral degradation nor unpatriotic self-consideration."—(*Nineteenth Century*, July, 1891, p. 84.)

8.—" . . . *the tinge of shame.*"

Why indeed should shame have attached specially to those women, more highly cultured and better treated than wives; and whose sole impeachment could be that they rejected the still lower serfdom of wedded bondage?

XIII.

2.—"*To him who fixed the gages of the fight.*"

"If we could imagine a Bossuet or a Fénélon figuring among the followers of Ninon de Lenclos, and publicly giving her counsel on the subject of her professional duties, and the means of securing adorers, this would be hardly less strange than the relation which really existed between Socrates and the courtesan Theodota."—Lecky ("History of European Morals," Vol. II., p. 280).

8.—"*The waste of woman worth*

Since these words were written, a letter from Mrs. Mona Caird has been published by the "Women's Emancipation Union," in which is said:—"So far from giving safety and balance to the 'natural forces,' these time-honoured restrictions, springing from a narrow theory which took its rise in a pre-scientific age, are fraught with the gravest dangers, creating a perpetual struggle and unrest, filling society with the perturbations and morbid developments of powers that ought to be spending themselves freely and healthfully on their natural objects. Any-one who has looked a little below the surface of women's lives can testify to the general unrest and nervous exhaustion or *malaise* among them, although each would probably refer her suffering to some cause peculiar to herself and her circumstances, never dreaming that she was the victim of an evil that gnaws at the very heart of society, making of almost every woman the heroine of a silent tragedy. I think few keen observers will deny that it is almost always the women of placid temperament, with very little sensibility, who are happy and contented; those of more highly wrought nervous systems and imaginative faculty, who are nevertheless capable of far greater joy than their calmer sisters, in nine cases out of ten are secretly intensely miserable. And the cause of this is not eternal and unalterable. The nervously organised being is *not* created to be miserable; but when intense vital energy is thwarted and misdirected—so long as the energy lasts—there must be intense suffering. . . . It is only when resignation sets in, when the ruling order convinces at last and tires out the rebel nerves and the keen intelligence, that we know that the living forces are defeated, and that death has come to quiet the suffering. All this is waste of human force, and far worse than waste."

Id. . . Alexandre Dumas fils says:—"Celles-là voient, de jour en jour, en sondant l'horizon toujours le même, s'effeuiller dans l'isolement, dans l'inaction, dans l'impuissance, les facultés divines qui leur avaient d'abord fait faire de si beaux rêves et dont il leur semble que l'expansion eût pu être matériellement et moralement si profitable aux autres et à elles-memes."—("Les Femmes qui Tuent et les Femmes qui Votent," p. 107).

Id. And Lady Florence Dixie has written:—"Nature gives strength and beauty to man, and Nature gives strength and beauty to woman. In this latter instance man flies in the face of Nature, and declares that she must be artificially restrained. Woman must not be allowed to grow up strong like man, because if she did the fact would establish her equality with him, and this cannot be tolerated.

So the boy and man are allowed freedom of body, and are trained up to become muscular and strong, while the woman, by artificial, not natural, laws, is bidden to remain inactive and passive, and, in consequence, weak and undeveloped. Mentally it is the same. Nature has unmistakably given to woman a greater amount of brain power. This is at once perceivable in childhood. For instance, on the stage, girls are always employed in preference to boys, for they are considered brighter and sharper in intellect and brain power. Yet man deliberately sets himself to stunt that early evidence of mental capacity by laying down the law that woman's education shall be on a lower level than that of man's; that natural truths, which all women should early learn, should be hidden from her; and that while men may be taught everything, women must only acquire a narrow and imperfect knowledge both of life and of Nature's laws. I maintain that this procedure is abitrary and cruel, and false to Nature. I characterise it by the strong word of infamous. It has been the means of sending to their graves, unknown, unknelled, and unnamed, thousands of women whose high intellects have been wasted, and whose powers for good have been paralysed and undeveloped."—("Gloriana: or, the Revolution of 1900," p. 130.)

Id. . . Buckle gives numerous instances which support the foregoing assertions, saying himself on the point:—"That women are more deductive than men, because they think quicker than men, is a proposition which some persons will not relish, and yet it may be proved in a variety of ways. Indeed, nothing could prevent its being universally admitted except the fact that the remarkable rapidity with which women think is obscured by that miserable, that contemptible, that preposterous system called their education, in which valuable things are carefully kept from them, and trifling things carefully taught to them, until their fine and nimble minds are irreparably injured."—("Miscellaneous Works," Vol. I., p. 8, "On the influence of Women on the Progress of Knowledge.")

Id. As a man of straightforward common-sense, Sydney Smith has left a name unsurpassed in our literary history. Here is something of what he says on this question of woman's intellect and its waste :—"As the matter stands at present, half the talent in the universe runs to waste, and is totally unprofitable. It would have been almost as well for the world, hitherto, that women, instead of possessing the capacities they do at present, should have been born wholly destitute of wit, genius, and every other attribute of mind of which men make so eminent a use; and the ideas of use and possession are so united together that, because it has been the custom in almost all countries to give to women a different and worse education than to men, the notion has obtained that they do not possess faculties which they do not cultivate."—("Essay on Female Education.")

Id. Hear also John Ruskin on the relative intellect or capacity of women :—"Let us try, then, whether we cannot get at some clear and harmonious idea (and it must be harmonious if it is true) of what womanly mind and virtue are in power and office, with respect to man's; and how their relations, rightly accepted, aid and increase the vigour, and honour, and authority of both. Let us see whether the greatest, the wisest, the purest-hearted of all ages are agreed in anywise on this point. . . . And first let us take Shakespeare; . . . there is hardly a play that has not a perfect woman in it, steadfast in grave hope and errorless purpose. . . Such, in broad light, is Shakespeare's testimony to the position and character of women in human life. He represents them as infallibly faithful and wise counsellors, incorruptibly just and pure examples, strong always to sanctify, even when they cannot save. . . . I ask you next to receive the witness of Walter Scott. . . . So that, in all cases, with Scott as with Shakespeare, it is the woman who watches over, teaches, and guides the youth; it is never, by any chance, the youth who watches over or educates his mistress.

"Now I could multiply witness upon witness of this kind upon you, if I had time. Nay, I could go back into the mythical teaching of the most ancient times, and show you how the great people, how that great Egyptian people, wisest then of nations, gave to their Spirit of Wisdom the form of a woman; and into her hand, for a symbol, the weaver's shuttle; and how the name and form of that spirit adopted, believed, and obeyed by the Greeks, became that Athena of the olive-helm and cloudy shield, to whose faith you owe, down to this date, whatever you hold most precious in art, in literature, or in types of national virtue.

"But I will not wander into this distant and mythical element; I will only ask you to give the legitimate value to the testimony of these great poets and men of the world, consistent as you see it is on this head. I will ask you whether it can be supposed that these men, in the main work of their lives, are amusing themselves with a fictitious and idle view of the relations between man and woman; nay, worse than fictitious or idle, for a thing may be imaginary yet desirable, if it were possible; but this, their ideal of women, is, according to our common idea of the marriage relation, wholly undesirable. The woman, we say, is not to guide nor even to think for herself. The man is always to be the wiser; he is to be the thinker, the ruler, the superior in knowledge and discretion, as in power. Is it not somewhat important to make up our minds on this matter? Are Shakespeare and Æschylus, Dante and Homer merely dressing dolls for us; or, worse than dolls, unnatural visions, the realisation of which, were it possible, would bring anarchy into all households, and ruin into all affections? Are all these great men mistaken, or, are we?"—("Sesame and Lilies," p. 125, *et seq.*)

Truly, in the face of these things, Tennyson had reason concerning his fellow men, when he wrote:—

"Knowledge comes, but wisdom lingers . . ."
("Locksley Hall.")

XIV.

3.— . . *lostling* . . .

Between the most cultured *hetairai* and the poor outcast as here shown, were many intervening or coalescing grades. Instance, as one of the phases, the following sketch of an Indian courtesan:—"Lalun is a member of the most ancient profession in the world. Lilith was her very-great-grandmama, and that was before the days of Eve, as everyone knows. In the West, people say rude things about Lalun's profession, and write lectures about it, and distribute the lectures to young people, in order that morality may be preserved. In the East, where the profession is hereditary, descending from mother to daughter, nobody writes lectures or takes any notice."—Rudyard Kipling ("On the City Wall").

Id.—" . . . *worse than brutal woes*

Dumas fils, who knew well whereof he wrote, tells of "Les femmes du peuple et de la campagne, suant du matin au soir pour gagner le pain quotidien, le dos courbé, domptées par la misère:" of whom some of the daughters "sortent du groupe par le chemin tentant et facile de la prostitution, mais où le labeur est encore plus rude."—("Les Femmes qui Tuent et les Femmes qui Votent," p. 101.) As historical instance of depth of wretched degradation, *conf.* mediæval privilege of "*scortum ante mortem*," conceded to some of even the vilest and lowest of criminals condemned to capital punishment. Though such a condition is barely more than parallel to the pitch of infamy of modern times, as instanced in a quotation reproduced by John Ruskin, in "Sesame and Lilies," p. 91, first ed.:—

"The salons of Mme. C., who did the honours with clever imitative grace and elegance, were crowded with princes, dukes, marquises, and counts, in fact, with the same *male* company as one meets at the parties of the Princess Metternich and Madame Drouyn de Lhuys. Some English peers and members of Parliament were present, and appeared to enjoy the animated and dazzlingly improper scene. On the second floor the supper-tables were loaded with every delicacy of the season. That your readers may form some idea of the dainty fare of the Parisian *demi-monde*, I copy the *menu* of the supper which was served to all the guests (about 200) seated, at four o'clock. Choice Yquem, Johannisberg, Lafitte, Tokay, and Champagne of the finest vintages were served most lavishly throughout the morning. After supper dancing was resumed with increased animation, and the ball terminated with a *chaine diabolique* and a *cancan d'enfer* at seven in the morning."—(*Morning Post*, March 10th, 1865.)

To which perhaps the most fitting comment is certain words of Letourneau's:—"It is important to make a distinction. The resemblance between the moral coarseness of the savage and the depravation of the civilised man is quite superficial. The brutality of the savage has nothing in common with the moral retrogression of the civilised man, struck with decay. . . . The posterity of the savage may, with the aid of time and culture, attain to great moral elevation, for there are vital forces within him which are fresh and intact. The primitive man is still young, and he possesses many latent energies susceptible of development. In short, the savage is a child, while the civilised man, whose moral nature is corrupt, presents to us rather the picture of decrepit old age."—("Evolution of Marriage," Chap. V.)

If M. Letourneau will apply his strictures as to senility and decay to so-called "Society" and its system, rather than to the individual, he will find many thinkers, both of his own and other nationalities, agree with his conclusion. Yet not death, but reform, is the righter event to indicate. And by what means that reform may be ensured is, at least in part, clearly set forth in the following passage from a paper recently published by the Women's Printing Society:—

"My positive belief is that women, and women alone, will be able to reverse the world's verdict, but they must change their method of reform in two important matters.

"First and foremost, every mother must teach her daughters the truth, the whole truth, and nothing but the truth about the relations of the sexes, the condition of social opinion, the historical, physiological, ethical aspects of the question. She must train herself so as to be able to teach the young minds these solemn, serious aspects of life, in such a way that the world may learn that the innocence of ignorance is inferior to the purity of right-minded, fearless knowledge. She must strengthen the minds and form the judgment of her daughters, so that they may demand reciprocal purity in those whom they would espouse.

"I fully understand the difficulty of teaching our pure-minded, delicately-nurtured daughters the terrible lessons of this seamy side of life. I am a mother of daughters myself, and I know the cost at which the courage has to be obtained, but in this matter each mother must help another. What a mighty force is influence! What help is conveyed by pressure of opinion! How often do I remember with gratitude the words which I once read as quoted of Mrs. John Stuart Mill, who taught her little daughter to have the courage to hear what other little girls had to bear. How gladly I acknowledge the stimulus of that example to myself, and therefore I would urge all women to SPEAK OUT. Do not be afraid. You will not lose your womanliness. You will not lose your purity. You will not have your sensibilities blunted by such rough use. No, "To the pure all things are pure." We must reach the mass through the unit, it is the individual who helps to move the world.

"We must teach and train the mind of every woman with whom we come in contact, for we have mighty work to do. A no less deed than to reverse the judgment of the whole world on the subject of purity. I do not believe it is possible for men to accomplish any radical reform in this matter. It belongs to women—I was going to say exclusively—but I will modify my assertion; and if women do not speak out more courageously in the future than they have done in the past, I believe there is but slight chance of any further amelioration in the condition of society than those which are such an inadequate return at the present time, for all the love and money expended on them."

And the same writer says, on a still more recent occasion: "I find no words strong enough to denounce the sin of silence amongst women on these social evils; and I have come to feel that the best proof of the subjection and degradation of my sex lies in the opinions often expressed by so-called Christian and pure women *about other women.* If their judgments were not perverted, if their wills were not broken, if their consciences were not asleep, and if their souls were not enslaved, they would not, they could not, hold their peace and let the havoc go on with women and children as it does."—Mrs. Laura E. Morgan-Browne ("*Woman's Herald*, 27th Feb., 1892).

Mrs. Morgan-Browne is, perhaps, not more than needfully severe on the almost criminal reticence of women; yet man must certainly take the greater share of blame for the social "double morality" which condemns irrevocably a woman, and leaves practically unscathed a man, for the same act. It is male-made laws and rules that have resulted in the perverted judgments, broken wills, sleeping consciences, and enslaved souls, which both sexes may deplore. Charles Kingsley pointed a cogent truth when he said that "Women will never obtain moral equity until they have civil equality." (See also Note XXXV., 6.)

XV.

2.— . . . *woman's griefs with man of barbarous breed.*"

"In all barbarous societies the subjection of woman is more or less severe; customs or coarse laws have regulated the savagery of the first anarchic ages; they have doubtless set up a barrier against primitive ferocity, they have interdicted certain absolutely terrible abuses of force, but they have only replaced these by a servitude which is still very heavy, is often iniquitous, and no longer permits to legally-possessed women those escapes, or capriciously accorded liberties, which were tolerated in savage life."—Letourneau (" Evolution of Marriage," Chap. XIV.).

4.—" *Crippled and crushed by cruelty and toil.*"

Some of this crippling has been of set purpose, as well as the simple result of brutal male recklessness. Instance the distortion of the feet of high-born female children in China, the tradition concerning which is that the practice was initiated and enjoined by an emperor of old, one of whose wives had (literally) "run away" from him. A somewhat similar precaution would seem to be indicated as a very probable source of the persistent and almost universal incommodity and incumbrance of the dress of woman as compared with that of man.

Dr. Thomas Inman, in his "Ancient Faiths Embodied in Ancient Names," Vol. I., p. 53, seems to indicate a different, yet closely allied, origin and motive for the impeding form of woman's clothing, the subordinate status of woman being always the purpose in view.

Id. "Even supposing a woman to give no encouragement to her admirers, many plots are always laid to carry her off. In the encounters which result from these, she is almost certain to receive some violent injury, for each of the combatants orders her to follow him, and, in the event of her refusing, throws a spear at her. The early life of a young woman at all celebrated for beauty is generally one continued series of captivities to different masters, of ghastly wounds, of wandering in strange families, of rapid flights, of bad treatment from other females amongst whom she is brought, a stranger, by her captor; and rarely do you see a form of unusual grace and elegance but it is marked and scarred by the furrows of old wounds; and many a female thus wanders several hundred miles from the home of her infancy, being carried off successively to distant and more distant points."—Sir George Grey ("Travels in North-Western Australia," 1841, Vol. II., p. 249; quoted in M'Lennan on "Primitive Marriage," p. 75).

5.—" *her heart a gentle mien essayed.*"

"Woman seems to differ from man in mental disposition, chiefly in greater tenderness and less selfishness, and this holds good even with savages, as shown by a well-known passage in "Mungo Park's Travels," and by statements made by other travellers. Woman, owing to her maternal instincts, displays these qualities towards her infants in an eminent degree; therefore it is likely that she should often extend them towards her fellow creatures." . . "Mungo Park heard the negro women teaching their young children to love the truth."—Darwin ("The Descent of Man," Chaps. IX., III.).

6.—"*By deeper passion, holier impulse, swayed.*"

Mrs. Eliza W. Farnham well says:—"Woman has accepted her subordinate lot, and lived in it with comparatively little moral harm, as the only truly superior and noble being could have done. The masculine spirit, enslaved and imprisoned, becomes diabolic or broken; the feminine, only warped, weakened, or distorted, is ready, whenever the pressure upon it is removed, to assume its true attitude."—("Woman and Her Era," Part IV.)

Id. Perhaps as appositely here, as elsewhere, may be recorded the following:—"An American writer says 'While I lived among the Choctaw Indians, I held a consultation with one of their chiefs respecting the successive stages of their progress in the arts of civilised life, and, among other things, he informed me that at their start they made a great mistake, they only sent boys to school. Their boys came home intelligent men, but they married uneducated and uncivilised wives, and the uniform result was that the children were all like their mothers. The father soon lost all his interest both in wife and children. And now,' said he, 'if we could educate but one class of our children, we should choose the girls, for, when they become mothers, they educate their sons.' This is the point, and it is true.'"—(*Manchester Examiner and Times*, Sept., 1870.)

8.—" *mother-love alone the infant oft preserved.*"

In Polynesia, "if a child was born, the husband was free to kill the infant, which was done by applying a piece of wet stuff to the mouth and nose, or to let it live; but, in the latter case, he generally kept the wife for the whole of her life. If the union was sterile, or the children put to death, the man had always the right to abandon the woman when and how it seemed good to him." —Letourneau ("Evolution of Marriage," p. 113).

Id. An Arab legend tells of a chief of Tamin, who became a constant practitioner of infanticide in consequence of a wound given to his pride . . . and from that moment he interred alive all his daughters, according to the ancient custom. But one day, during his absence, a daughter was born to him, whom the mother secretly sent to a relative to save her, and then declared to her husband that she had been delivered of a still-born child.—(R. Smith, on "Kinship," p. 282; quoted by Letourneau, "Evolution of Marriage," p. 83.)

Id. Charles Darwin writes of Tierra del Fuego:— "The husband is to the wife a brutal master to a laborious slave. Was a more horrid deed ever perpetrated than that witnessed on the west coast by Byron, who saw a wretched mother pick up her bleeding, dying infant-boy, whom her husband had mercilessly dashed on the stones for dropping a basket of sea-eggs!"—("Voyage of the *Beagle*," Chap. X.)

Id. . . Mrs. Reichardt tells of a certain Moslem, of high standing in the society of Damascus, who "married a young girl of ten, and, after she had born him two sons, he drove her almost mad with such cruelty and unkindness that she escaped, and went back to her father. Her husband sent for her to return, and, as she was hidden out of his sight, he wrung the necks of both his sons, and sent their bodies to his wife to show her what he had in store for her. The young mother, not yet twenty, died in a few days."—(See *Nineteenth Century*, June, 1891.)

Id. . It will not be forgotten that, in more than one

of the older civilisations, the father had the power of life and death over the members of the family, even past adult age.

And, to come to quite recent times, and this our England, Mrs. Wolstenholme Elmy, to whose unflagging energy, during some fifteen years of labour, was mainly attributable (as the Parliamentary sponsors of the measures know) the amelioration in the English law concerning wives and mothers, embodied in the Married Women's Property Acts of 1870 and 1882, together with the later and beneficent Guardianship of Infants Act, 1886, relates, in her record of the history of this latter Act:—

"It will be remembered that so recently as 1883, a young lady petitioned that she might be allowed to spend her summer holidays with her own mother, from whom she was separated for no fault of her own or of her mother's, but in virtue of the supreme legal rights of her father. The Court refused her petition, natural and proper as it seems to everyone of human feelings; and the words of the Master of the Rolls in giving judgment, on the 24th of July, 1883, are more significant and instructive as to the actual state of the law than the words of any non-professional writer can be:—'The law of England *recognises the rights of the father*, not as the guardian, but *because he is the father of his children. . . . The rights of the father are recognised because he is the father;* his duties as a father are recognised because they are natural duties. The natural duties of a father are to treat his children with the utmost affection, and with infinite tenderness. . . . The law recognises these duties, from which if a father breaks he breaks from everything which nature calls upon him to do; and, although the law may not be able to insist upon their performance, it is because the law recognises them, and knows that in almost every case the natural feelings of a father will prevail. The law trusts that the father will perform his natural duties, and does not, and, indeed, cannot, inquire how they have been performed. . I am not prepared to say whether *when the child is a ward of Court, and the conduct of the father is such as to exhaust all patience—such, for instance, as cruelty, or pitiless spitefulness carried to a great extent—the Court might not interfere. But such interference will be exercised* ONLY IN THE UTMOST NEED, AND IN MOST EXTREME CASES. It is impossible to lay down the rule of the Court more clearly than ha been done by Vice-Chancellor Bacon in the recent case of "*Re* Plowley" (47 "L.T.," N.S., 283). In saying that this Court, "whatever be its authority or jurisdiction, *has no authority to interfere with the sacred right of a father over his own children*," the learned Vice-Chancellor has summed up all that I intended to say. *The rights of a father are sacred rights, because his duties are sacred.* . . .'

"These sacred rights of the father were, it will be observed, in the eyes of the law so *exclusive* and paramount as to justify and demand the refusal to a young girl, at the most critical period of early womanhood, of the solace of a few weeks' intercourse with a blameless and beloved mother ; and this although the gratification of the daughter's wish would have involved no denial to the father of the solace of his daughter's company, since she was not actually, but only *legally*, in his custody, not having seen him for more than a year.

"It will be seen from this that the father alone has the absolute legal right to deal with his child or children, to the extent of separating them, at his own sole pleasure, from their mother, and of giving them into the care and custody of any person whom he may think fit. The mother has, as such, no legal status, no choice, voice, lot, or part in the matter."—Mrs. Wolstenholme Elmy ("The Infants' Act, 1886," p. 2).

It is consolatory to learn that a palliation of some part of the above unjust conditions has been achieved; yet how often has our presumedly happy land witnessed scenes of child misery and helpless mother-love, to which was denied even the poor consolation, so pathetically depicted by Mrs. Browning, in a scene which, as Moir truly says, "weighs on the heart like a nightmare";—

"Do you hear the children weeping, oh! my brothers!
Ere the sorrow comes with years?
They are leaning their young heads against their mothers,
And *that* cannot stop their tears."

XVI.

4.—" . . . . *single basis*

First written "disproportioned basis," but altered, with good reason, in the face of Mr. Herbert Spencer's arrogant male thesis:—" Only that mental energy is normally feminine which can co-exist with the production and nursing of the due (!) number of healthy children."—(" Study of Sociology," Chap. XV., note 5.)

But Professor Huxley speaks, more humanly, of " such a peasant woman as one sees in the Alps, striding ever upward, heavily burdened, and with mind bent only on her home; but yet, without effort and without thought, knitting for her children. Now stockings are good and comfortable things, and the children will undoubtedly be much the better for them, but surely it would be short-sighted, to say the least of it, to depreciate this toiling mother as a mere stocking-machine—a mere provider of physical comforts." —(" On Improving Natural Knowledge.")

Yet, if it be—as truly it is—a senseless aud disgraceful depreciation of woman to look upon her as "a mere machine for the making of stockings," is it not equally unworthy and unwise to consider her as—primarily and essentially—a mere machine for the making of a "due" number of stocking-wearers?

5.—" . . . *quicker fire.*"

In even so sedate and usually dispassionate a physiologist and philosopher as Charles Darwin, the masculine sex-bias is so ingrained and so ingenuous that he strives to disparage and contemn the notorious mental quickness or intuition of woman by saying :—"It is generally admitted that with woman the powers of intuition, of rapid perception, and perhaps of imitation, are more strongly marked than in man; but some, at least, of these faculties are characteristic of the lower races, and therefore of a past and lower state of civilisation."—("The Descent of Man," Chap. XIX.).

His unconscious sex-bias apparently overlooked the pregnant and very pertinent caution which he had himself uttered in a previous work :—"Useful organs, however little they may be developed, unless we have reason to suppose that they were formerly more highly developed, ought not to be considered as rudimentary. They may be in a nascent condition, and in progress towards further development. Rudimentary organs, on the other hand, are either quite useless, such as teeth which never cut through the gums, or, almost useless, such as the wings of an ostrich, which serve merely as sails. . . . It is, however, often difficult to distinguish between rudimentary and nascent organs, for we can judge only by analogy whether a part is capable of further development, in which case alone it deserves to be called nascent."—("Origin of Species," Chap. XIV.).

But surely Darwin would admit that experiment in capacity of education and development was as worthy evidence as "analogy," and would further acknowledge how little effort in this direction had ever been made with woman. Buckle would seem to be far nearer the truth in ascribing to woman an unconscious deductive form of reasoning, as against the slow and studied inductive process to which man is so generally trained to be a slave.—(See Buckle's Essay on the "Influence of Women on the Progress of Knowledge," as quoted from in Note XIII., 8.)

7.—" *one permitted end* . . ."

"The function of child-bearing has been exaggerated to an utterly disproportionate degree in her life; it has been made her almost sole claim to existence. Yet it is not the true purpose of any intellectual organism to live solely to give birth to succeeding organisms; its duty is also to live for its own happiness and well-being."—Ben Elmy ("Studies in Materialism," Chap. III.).

Id. " . . . not a moth with vain desire
Is shrivelled in a fruitless fire,
Or but subserves another's gain."
—Tennyson ("In Memoriam," LIV).

XVII.

5.—" . . *aspirations crushed*

"I have found life a series of hopes unfulfilled and wishes ungratified."—(Dying words of a talented woman.)

6.—" . . . *purblind pride* . . ."

"Pride, where wit fails, steps in to our defence,
And fills up all the mighty void of sense."
—Pope.

7.—" *Her every wish made subject*

For a somewhat modern exemplification may be taken

the instance of Elizabeth Barrett Browning, in Paris with her husband, in 1852. She writes of Georges Sand :—"She received us in a room with a bed in it, the only room she has to occupy, I suppose, during her short stay in Paris. . . . Ah, but I didn't see her smoke ; I was unfortunate. I could only go with Robert three times to her house, and once she was out. He was really very good and kind to let me go at all after he found the sort of society rampant around her. He didn't like it extremely, but, being the prince of husbands, he was lenient to my desires, and yielded the point."—("Life of Robert Browning," by Mrs. Sutherland Orr, 1891.)

8.—" . . . *her God.*"

Conf. Milton ("Paradise Lost," Book IV., 299) :—

"He for God only, she for God in him."

See Note XXXV., 5. Compare also the Code of Manu, v. 154, as quoted by Letourneau :—"Although the conduct of her husband may be blameworthy, and he may give himself up to other amours, and be devoid of good qualities, a virtuous woman ought constantly to revere him as a God." —("Evolution of Marriage," Chap. XIII.)

Id. . . Here may fittingly be appended some masculine concepts of feminine duty in other races.

The STATUS OF WOMAN, according to the CHINESE Classics :—

In a periodical published in Shanghai, Dr. Faber, a well-known scholar, writes (1891) a paper on the status of women in China. He refers especially to the theoretical position assigned to women by the Chinese Classics. These lay down the different dogmas on the subject:

"1.—Women are as different in nature from man as earth is from heaven.

"2.—Dualism, not only in body form, but in the very essence of nature, is indicated and proclaimed by Chinese moralists of all times and creed. The male belongs to *yang*, the female to *yin*.

"3.—Death and all other evils have their origin in the *yin*, or female principle; life and prosperity come from its subjection to the *yang* or male principle; and it is therefore regarded as a law of nature that women should be kept under the control of men, and not be allowed any will of their own.

"4.—Women, indeed, are human beings, (!) but they are of a lower state than men, and can never attain to full equality with them.

"5.—The aim of female education, therefore, is perfect submission, not cultivation and development of mind.

"6.—Women cannot have any happiness of their own; they have to live and work for men.

"7.—Only as the mother of a son, as the continuator of the direct line of a family, can a woman escape from her degradation and become to a certain degree her husband's equal; but then only in household affairs, especially the female department, and in the ancestral hall.

"8.—In the other world, woman's condition remains exactly the same, for the same laws of existence apply. She is not the equal of her husband; she belongs to him, and is dependent for her happiness on the sacrifice offered by her descendants.

"These are the doctrines taught by Confucius, Mencius, and the ancient sages, whose memory has been revered in China for thousands of years."

And now, what wonder that Chinese civilisation and progress is, and remains, fossilised, inert, dead?

JAPAN.

"There is one supreme maxim upon which the conduct of a well-bred woman is made to turn, and this is 'obedience.' Life, the Japanese girl is taught, divides itself into three stages of obedience. In youth she is to obey her father; in marriage her husband; in widowhood her eldest son. Hence her preparation for life is always preparation for service. The marriage of the Japanese girl usually takes place when she is about seventeen. It is contrary to all custom that she should have any voice in it. Once married, she passes from her father's household into the household of her husband, and her period of self-abnegation begins. Her own family is to be as nothing to her. Her duty is to charm the existence of her husband, and to please his relations. Custom demands that she shall always smile upon him, and that she shall carefully hide from him any signs of bad humour, jealousy, or physical pain."—Tinseau (quoted in *Review of Reviews*, Vol. IV., p. 282.)

Note well the last two words of the above quotation; they have a bearing on much that will have to be said presently. Meanwhile, we read from another writer: "The expression, *res angusta domi*, might have been invented for Japan, so narrow of necessity is the wife's home life. The husband mixes with the world, the wife does not; the husband has been somewhat inspired, and his thoughts widened by his intercourse with foreigners, the wife has not met them. The husband has more or less acquaintance with western learning; the wife has none. Affection between the two, within the limits which unequal intellectuality ruthlessly prescribes, there well may be, but the love which comes of a perfect intimacy, of mutual knowledge and common aspiration, there can rarely be. The very vocabulary of romantic love does not exist in Japanese; *a fortiori*, there is little of the fact." Yet, under the influence of western civilisation, these things are changing rapidly, and Mr. Norman, the commissioner of the *Pall Mall Gazette*, further relates that "The generation that is now growing up will be very different. Not only will the men of it be more western, but the women also. As girls they will have been to schools like our schools at home, and they will have learned English, and history, and geography, and science, and foreign music; perhaps, even, something of politics and political economy. They will know something of 'society,' as we now use the term, and will both seek it and make it. The old home-life will become unbearable to the woman, and she will demand the right of choosing her husband just as much as he chooses her. Then the rest will be easy."

The harsh and restrained position, both of Japanese and Chinese women, is frequently attributed to Confucianism; yet the matter does not seem to be of any one creed, but rather of every religious creed. Thus Mrs. Reichardt tells us, concerning Mahommedan women and Mahommedan married life, that—

"A Mahommedan girl is brought up with the idea that she has nothing to do with love. It is *ayib* (shame) for her to love her husband. She dare not do it if she would. What he asks and expects of her is to tremble before him, and yield him unquestioning obedience. I have *seen* a husband look pleased and complacent when his wife looked afraid to lift up her eyes, even when visitors were present."—(*Nineteenth Century*, June, 1891.)

Nor is Confucius alone, or the simple contagion of his teaching, rightly to be blamed for the following condition of things in our own dependency of

INDIA.

The *Bombay Guardian* calls attention to an extraordinary book which is being circulated (early in 1891) broadcast, as a prize-book in the Government Girls' School in the Bombay Presidency The following quotations are given as specimens of the teachings set forth in the book:—

"If the husband of a virtuous woman be ugly, of good or bad disposition, diseased, fiendish, irascible, or a drunkard, old, stupid, dumb, blind, deaf, hot-tempered, poor, extremely covetous, a slanderer, cowardly, perfidious, and immoral, nevertheless she ought to worship him as God, with mind, speech, and person.

"The wife who gives an angry answer to her husband will become a village pariah dog; she will also become a jackal, and live in an uninhabited desert.

"The woman who eats sweetmeats without sharing them with her husband will become a hen-owl, living in a hollow tree.—(*Conf.* Note VI., 8.)

"The woman who walks alone without her husband will become a filth-eating village sow.

"The woman who speaks disrespectfully to her husband will be dumb in the next incarnation.

"The woman who hates her husband's relations will become from birth to birth a musk-rat, living in filth.

"She who is always jealous of her husband's concubine will be childless in the next incarnation."

To illustrate the blessed result of a wife's subserviency, a story is told of "the great reward that came to the wife of an ill-tempered, diseased, and wicked Brahmin, who served her husband with a slavish obedience, and even went the length of carrying him on her own shoulders to visit his mistress."

So quotes the *Woman's Journal* of Boston, Mass., and says in comment thereon:—"The British Government in India has bound itself not to interfere with the religion of the natives, but it certainly ought not to inculcate in Government schools the worst doctrines of heathenism."

Yet, again, are these Hindoo, or Japanese, or Chinese doctrines simply the precepts of "heathenism" alone? Buckle quotes for us the following passage from the Nonconformist, "Fergusson on the Epistles," 1656, p. 242:—"There is not any husband to whom this honour of submission is not due. No personal infirmity, frowardness of nature, no, not even on the point of religion, doth deprive him of it."

Much the same teaching is continued a century later in the noted Dr. Gregory's "A Father's Legacy to his Daughters"; and again, hideously true is the picture which Mill has to draw, in 1869:—"Above all, a female slave has (in Christian countries) an admitted right, and is considered under a moral obligation to refuse to her master the last familiarity. Not so the wife; however brutal a tyrant she may unfortunately be chained to, though she may know that he hates her, though it may be his daily pleasure to torture her, and though she may feel it impossible not to loathe him, he can claim from her and enforce the lowest degradation of a human being, that of being made the instrument of an animal function contrary to her inclinations. No amount of ill-usage, without adultery superadded, will in England free a wife from her tormentor."—("The Subjection of Women," pp. 57, 59.)

As to how far public feeling, if not law, has amended some of these conditions, see Note XXXVI., 6. Meanwhile, as an evidence of what is the "orthodox" opinion and sentiment at this present day, it may be noted that Cardinal Manning wrote in the *Dublin Review*, July, 1891:—"A woman enters for life into a sacred contract with a man before God at the altar to fulfil to him the duties of wife, mother, and head of his home. Is it lawful for her, even with his consent, to make afterwards a second contract for so many shillings a week with a millowner whereby she becomes unable to provide her husband's food, train up her children, or do the duties of her home? It is no question of the lawfulness of gaining a few more shillings for the expenses of a family, but of the lawfulness of breaking a prior contract, the most solemn between man and woman. No arguments of expediency can be admitted. It is an obligation of conscience to which all things must give way. The duties of home must first be done" (by the woman) "then other questions may be entertained."

Are not these English injunctions to womanly and wifely slavery as trenchant and merciless as any ascribed to so-called "heathenism"? And is it not the fuller truth that the spirit of the male teaching against woman is the same all the world over, and no mere matter of creed—which is nevertheless made the convenient vehicle for such teaching; and that, in brief, the precepts of womanly and wifely servitude are blind, brutal, and universal?

See also Note XXXIV., 8.

XVIII.

8.—"*To compass power unknown in body and in mind.*"

"We need a new ethic of the sexes, and this not merely, or even mainly, as an intellectual construction, but as a discipline of life, and we need more. We need an increasing education and civism of women."—P. Geddes and J. A. Thomson ("The Evolution of Sex," p. 297).

Newnham and Girton, Vassar and Zurich, are already rendering account of woman's scope of mental power; while the circus, the gymnasium, swimming and mountaineering are showing what she might do corporeally, apart from her hideous and literally impeding style of clothing. As for some other forms of utilitarian occupation, read the following concerning certain of the Lancashire women :—

"Mr. Edgar L. Wakeman, an observant American author, is at present on a visit to this country, and is giving his countrymen the benefit of his impressions of English life and social conditions.

"The 'pit-brow' lasses of the Wigan district will not need to complain, for he writes of them not only in a kindly spirit, but even with enthusiasm for their healthy looks, graceful figures, and good conduct. We need not follow his description of the processes in which the women of the colliery are employed, but we may say in passing that Mr. Wakeman was astonished by the 'wonderful quickness of eye and movement' shown by the 'screeners,' and by the 'superb physical development' and agility of the 'fillers.' He had expected to find them 'the most forlorn creatures bearing the image of women,' and he found them strong, healthy, good-natured, and thoroughly respectable. English roses glow from English cheeks. You cannot find plumper figures, prettier forms, more shapely necks, or daintier feet, despite the ugly clogs, in all of dreamful Andalusia. The "broo gear" is laid aside on the return home from work, and then the "pit-brow" lass is arrayed as becomingly as any of her class in England, and in the village street, or at church of a Sunday, you could not pick her out from among her companions, unless for her fine colour, form, and a positively classic poise and grace of carriage possessed by no other working women of England.

Altogether,' he says, 'I should seriously regard the pit-brow lasses as the handsomest, healthiest, happiest, and most respectable working women in England." —(*Manchester Guardian*, Aug. 28, 1891.)

Id. Concerning the question of male and female dress, evidence as to how far woman has been hindered and "handicapped" by her conventional attire, and not by her want of physical strength or courage, is reported from time to time in the public prints, as witness the following, published generally in the English newspapers of 14th Oct., 1891:—

"Not long since a well-known European courier, having grown grey in his occupation, fell ill, and like others similarly afflicted, was compelled to call in a doctor. This gentleman was completely taken by surprise on discovering that his patient was a female. Then the sick woman—who had piloted numerous English and American families through the land of the Latin, the Turk, and others, and led timid tourists safely through many imaginary dangers—confessed that she had worn men's clothes for forty years. She stated that her reasons for this masquerade were that having, at the age of thirteen, been left a friendless orphan, she had become convinced, after futile struggling for employment, that many of the obstacles in her path could be swept away by discarding her proper garments and assuming the *rôle* and attire of masculine youth. This she did. She closely cut her hair, bought boy's clothes, put them on, and sallied forth in the world to seek her fortune. With the change of dress seems to have come a change of luck, for she quickly found employment, and being an apt scholar, and facile at learning languages, was enabled after a time to obtain a position as courier, and, but for her unfortunate illness, it is tolerably certain that the truth would never have been revealed during her lifetime."

In the early days of April, 1892, the Vienna correspondent of the *Standard* reported that—

"On the 30th ult., there died in Hungary, at about the same hour, two ladies who served in 1848 in the Revolutionary Army, and fought in several of the fiercest battles, dressed in military uniform. One of them was several times promoted, and, under the name of Karl, attained the rank of First Lieutenant of Hussars. At this point, however, an artillery major stopped her military career by marrying her. The other fought under the name of Josef, and was decorated for valour in the field. She married long after the campaign. A Hungarian paper, referring to the two cases, says that about a dozen women fought in 1848 in the insurrectionary ranks."

Somewhat more detailed particulars concerning "Lieutenant Karl" were afterwards given by the *Manchester Guardian* (June 6, 1892), as follows :—

"The Austrian *Volkszeitung* announces the death of Frau Marie Hoche, who has had a most singular and romantic career. Her maiden name was Lepstuk. In the momentous year of 1848 Marie Lepstuk, who was then eighteen years of age, joined the German legion at Vienna ; then, returning home, she adopted the name of Karl and joined the Tyroler Jager Regiment of the revolutionary army. She showed great bravery in the battlefield, received the medallion, and was raised to the rank of lieutenant. A wound compelled her to go into hospital, but after her recovery she joined the Hussars. As a reward for exceeding bravery she was next made oberlieutenant on the field. Soon after this her sex was discovered, but a major fell in love with her, and they were married. At Vilagos both were taken prisoners, and while in the fortress she gave birth to her first child. After the major's death she was remarried to Oberlieutenant Hoche. For the past few years Frau Hoche has been in needy circumstances, but an appeal from Jokai brought relief."

All of which goes far to discredit M. Michelet's theory that women are "born invalids," an assertion which Dr. Julia Mitchell "stigmatises naturally enough as 'all nonsense,'" and is thus approved—with a strange magnanimity

—by the *British Medical Journal.*—(See *Pall Mall Gazette,* April 29, 1892.)

The "incapacity of women for military service" has been of late days continually quoted as a bar to their right of citizenship, as far as the Parliamentary Franchise is concerned. In the face of the foregoing cases, and of the fact that every mother risks her life in becoming a mother, while very few men, indeed, risk theirs on the battlefield, it might be thought that the fallacious argument would have perished from shame and inanition long ago. But the inconsistencies of partly-cultivated, masculine, one-sexed intellect are as stubborn as blind.

See also Note XLV., 6.

XIX.

6.—" *The ecstasy of earnest souls*

"Without recognising the possibilities of individual and of racial evolution, we are shut up to the conventional view that the poet and his heroine alike are exceptional creations, hopelessly beyond the everyday average of the race. Whereas, admitting the theory of evolution, we are not only entitled to the hope, but logically compelled to the assurance that these rare fruits of an apparently more than earthly paradise of love, which only the forerunners of the race have been privileged to gather, or, it may be, to see from distant heights, are yet the realities of a daily life towards which we and ours may journey."—Geddes and Thomson ("Evolution of Sex," p. 267).

Id. . . . "What marriage may be in the case of two

persons of cultivated faculties, identical in opinions and purposes, between whom there exists that best kind of equality, similarity of powers, and capacities with reciprocal superiority in them—so that each can enjoy the pleasure of looking up to the other, and can have alternately the pleasure of leading and of being led in the path of development—I will not attempt to describe. To those who can conceive it there is no need; to those who cannot, it would appear the dream of an enthusiast. But I maintain, with the profoundest conviction, that this, and this only, is the ideal of marriage; and that all opinions, customs, and institutions which favour any other notion of it, or turn the conceptions and aspirations connected with it into any other direction, by whatever pretences they may be coloured, are relics of primitive barbarism. The moral regeneration of mankind will only really commence when the most fundamental of the social relations is placed under the rule of equal justice, and when human beings learn to cultivate their strongest sympathy with an equal in rights and cultivation."—J. S. Mill ("The Subjection of Women," p. 177).

XX.

2.—"*And lingers still the hovering shade of night.*"

George Eliot had yet to say, "Heaven was very cruel when it made women"; and Georges Sand, "Fille on nous supprime, femme on nous opprime."

XXI.

1.—" *carnal servitude*

It may be objected by some that details in the verse or

in these notes are of too intimate a character for general narration. The notes have, however, all been taken either from widely read public prints of indisputable singleness of purpose, or works of writers of undoubted integrity. One is not much troubled as to those who would criticise further. To them may be offered the incident and words of the late Dr. Magee, who, as Bishop of Peterborough, and a member of a legislative committee on the question of child-life insurance, said:—"In this matter we have to count with two things: first, almost all our facts are secrets of the bed-chamber; and, secondly, we are opposed by great vested interests. This thing is not to be done without a good deal of pain."—(*Review of Reviews*, Vol. IV., p. 37).

And thus are verified, in a transcendental sense also, the words of Schiller:—

"Und *in feurigem Bewegen*
Werden alle Kräfte kund."

("Die Glocke.")

7.—"*Survival from dim age* "

See Note XXIII., 1.

XXII.

1.— . . . *girlhood's helpless years* . "

Somewhat as to these ancient conditions may be gathered from the position in India at the present day. Read the following:—"The practice of early marriages by Hindoos I was, of course, informed of by reading before coming to India, but its mention in books was always coupled with the assertion that in India girls reach puberty at a much earlier age than in cold climates. Judge, therefore, of my surprise to find that so far from Hindoo girls being precocious in physical development, they are much behind in this respect; that a Hindoo girl of fifteen is about the equal of an English child of eleven, instead of the reverse, and that the statements made to the contrary by Englishmen who have no opportunity of becoming acquainted with Hindoo family life, were totally misleading. In the first place they were under the impression that marriage never takes place before puberty, and, secondly, they accepted the Hindoo view as to what constitutes puberty. You know that, unfortunately, they were misled as regards the first point. I hope to show you that in the second place the idea which they accepted as correct is a totally mistaken one." —Mrs. Pechey Phipson, M.D. (Address to the Hindoos of Bombay on the subject of child-marriage; delivered at the Hall of the Prarthana Somaj, Bombay, on the 11th Oct., 1890).

2.— . . . *sexual wrong.*"

"As regards the marriage of girls before even what is called puberty, I can hardly trust myself to speak, so strongly are my feelings those of all Western—may I not say of all civilised?—people in looking upon it as actually criminal. Ah! gentlemen, those of you who are conversant with such cases as I have seen, cases like those of Phulmoni Dossee, which has just now stirred your hearts to insist upon some change in the existing law, and others where a life-long decrepitude has followed, to which death itself were far preferable, do you not feel with me that penal servitude is not too hard a punishment for such brutality? I am glad to think that a very large section of Hindoo men think with me. I have been repeatedly spoken to on the subject, and members even of those castes which are most guilty in this matter, have expressed to me a wish that Government would interfere and put a stop to the practice." —Mrs. Pechey Phipson, M.D., *op. cit.*

A terrible evidence to the evil is borne by the following document:—

[FROM "THE TIMES OF INDIA," NOVEMBER 8TH, 1890.]

To his Excellency the Viceroy and Governor-General of India.

May it please Your Excellency.—The undersigned ladies, practising medicine in India, respectfully crave your Excellency's attention to the following facts and considerations:—

1. Your Excellency is aware that the present state of the Indian law permits marriages to be consummated not only before the wife is physically qualified for the duties of maternity, but before she is able to perform the duties of the conjugal relation, thus giving rise to numerous and great evils.

2. This marriage practice has become the cause of gross immoralities and cruelties, which, owing to existing legislation, come practically under the protection of the law. In some cases the law has permitted homicide, and protected men, who, under other circumstances, would have been criminally punished.

3. The institution of child-marriage rests upon public sentiment, vitiated by degenerate religious customs and misinterpretation of religious books. There are thousands among the better educated classes who would rejoice if Government would take the initiative, and make such a law as your memorialists plead for, and in the end the masses would be grateful for their deliverance from the galling yoke that has bound them to poverty, superstition, and the slavery of custom for centuries

4. The present system of child-marriage, in addition to the physical and moral effects which the Indian Governments have deplored, produces sterility, and consequently becomes an excuse for the introduction of other child-wives into the family, thus becoming a justification for *polygamy*.

5. This system panders to sensuality, lowers the standard of health and morals, degrades the race, and tends to perpetuate itself and all its attendant evils to future generations.

6. The lamentable case of the child-wife, Phulmani Dassi, of Calcutta, which has excited the sympathy and the righteous indignation of the Indian public, is only one of thousands of cases that are continually happening, the final results being quite as horrible, but sometimes less immediate. The following instances have come under the personal observation of one or another of your Excellency's petitioners :—

A. Aged 9. Day after marriage. Left *femur* dislocated, *pelvis* crushed out of shape, flesh hanging in shreds.

B. Aged 10. Unable to stand, bleeding profusely, flesh much lacerated.

C. Aged 9. So completely ravished as to be almost beyond surgical repair. Her husband had two other living wives, and spoke very fine English.

D. Aged 10. A very small child, and entirely undeveloped physically. This child was bleeding to death from the *rectum*. Her husband was a man of about 40 years of age, weighing not less than 11 stone. He had accomplished his desire in an unnatural way.

E. Aged about 9. Lower limbs completely paralysed.

F. Aged about 12. Laceration of the *perineum* extending through the *sphincter ani*.

G. Aged about 10. Very weak from loss of blood. Stated that great violence had been done her in an unnatural way.

H. Aged about 12. Pregnant, delivered by *craniotomy* with great difficulty, on account of the immature state of the *pelvis* and maternal passage.

I. Aged about 7. Living with husband. Died in great agony after three days.

K. Aged about 10. Condition most pitiable. After one day in hospital was demanded by her husband for his "lawful" use, he said.

L. Aged 11. From great violence done her person will be a cripple for life. No use of her lower extremities.

M. Aged about 10. Crawled to hospital on her hands and knees. Has never been able to stand erect since her marriage.

N. Aged 9. Dislocation of *pubic arch*, and unable to stand, or to put one foot before the other

In view of the above facts, the undersigned lady doctors and medical practitioners appeal to your Excellency's compassion to enact or introduce a measure by which the consummation of marriage will not be permitted before the wife has attained the full age of fourteen (14) years. The undersigned venture to trust that the terrible urgency of the matter will be accepted as an excuse for this interruption of your Excellency's time and attention.

(Signed by 55 lady-physicians.)

The memorial as above was initiated by Mrs. Monelle Mansell, M.A., M.D., who has been in practice in India for seventeen years, and it received the signature of every other lady doctor there. The cases of abuse above specified are "only a few out of many hundreds—of cruel wrongs, deaths, and maimings for life received by helpless child-wives at the hands of brutal husbands, which have come under Dr. Monelle Mansell's personal observation, or that of her associates."

With regard to case K, and "lawful" use, compare what is said by Dr. Emma B. Ryder, who is also in medical practice in India, concerning the "Little Wives of India":

—"If I could take my readers with me on my round of visits for one week, and let them behold the condition of the little wives . . . if you could see the suffering faces of the little girls, who are drawn nearly double with contractions caused by the brutality of their husbands, and who will never be able to stand erect; if you could see the paralysed limbs that will not again move in obedience to the will; if you could hear the plaintive wail of the little sufferers as, with their tiny hands clasped, they beg you 'to make them die,' and then turn and listen to the brutal remarks of the legal owner with regard to the condition of his property. If you could stand with me by the side of the little deformed dead body, and, turning from the sickening sight, could be shown the new victim to whom the brute was already betrothed, do you think it would require long arguments to convince you that there was a deadly wrong somewhere, and that someone was responsible for it? After one such scene a Hindoo husband said to me, 'You look like feel bad' (meaning sad); 'doctors ought not to care what see. I don't care what see, nothing trouble me, only when self sick; I not like to have pain self.' A man may be a vile and loathsome creature, he may be blind, a lunatic, an idiot, a leper, or diseased in a worse form; he may be fifty, seventy, or a hundred years old, and may be married to a baby or a girl of five or ten, who positively loathes his presence, but if he claims her she must go, and the English law for the 'Restitution of Conjugal Rights' compels her to remain in his power, or imprisons her if she refuses. There is no other form of slavery on the face of the earth that begins with the slavery as enforced upon these little girls of

India."—("The Home-Maker," New York, June, 1891, quoted in the *Review of Reviews*, Vol. IV., p. 38.)

And the *Times* of 11th November, 1889, reported from its Calcutta correspondent:—"Two shocking cases of wife-killing lately came before the courts—in both cases the result of child-marriage. In one a child aged ten was strangled by her husband. In the second case a child of ten years was ripped open with a wooden peg. Brutal sexual exasperation was the sole apparent reason in both instances. Compared with the terrible evils of child-marriage, widow cremation is of infinitely inferior magnitude. The public conscience is continually being affronted with these horrible atrocities, but, unfortunately, native public opinion generally seems to accept these revelations with complete apathy."

For what slight legislative amendment has recently been effected in the grievances mentioned by Dr. Ryder, see Note XXIV., 4. The "Restitution of Conjugal Rights," so justly condemned by her, does, indeed, appear to have had—by some inadvertence—a recognition in the Indian Courts which was not its lawful due. But for some fuller particulars on this matter, both as concerns India and England, see Note XXXVI., 6.

XXIII.

1.—"*Action repeated tends to rhythmic course.*"

"Other and wider muscular actions, partly internal and partly external, also take place in a rhythmical manner in relation with systemic conditions. The motions of the diaphragm and of the thoracic and abdominal walls, in connection with respiration, belong to this category. These movements, though in the main independent of will, are capable of being very considerably modified thereby, and while they are most frequently unheeded, they have a very recognisable accompaniment of feeling when attention is distinctly turned to them. . . . The contraction of oviducts or of the womb, as well as the movements concerned in respiration, also had their beginnings in forms of life whose advent is now buried in the immeasurable past." —Dr. H. C. Bastian ("The Brain as an Organ of Mind," p. 220).

4.—"*Till habit bred hereditary trace.*"

"Let it be granted that the more frequently psychical states occur in a certain order, the stronger becomes their tendency to cohere in that order, until they at last become inseparable; let it be granted that this tendency is, in however slight a degree, inherited, so that if the experiences remain the same, each successive generation bequeaths a somewhat increased tendency, and it follows that, in cases like the one described, there must eventually result an automatic connection of nervous actions, corresponding to the external relations perpetually experienced. Similarly, if from some change in the environment of any species its members are frequently brought in contact with a relation having terms a little more involved; if the organisation of the species is so far developed as to be impressible by these terms in close succession, then an inner relation corresponding to this new outer relation will gradually be formed, and will, in the end, become organic. And so on in subsequent stages of progress."—Herbert Spencer ("Principles of Psychology," Vol. I., p. 439).

Id. . . . "I have described the manner in which the hereditary tendencies and instincts arise from habit, induced in the nervous cellules by a sufficient repetition of the same acts."—Letourneau ("The Evolution of Marriage," Chap. I.).

Id. . . . "Ainsi l'évacuation menstruelle une fois introduite dans l'espèce, se sera communiquée par une filiation non interrompue; de sorte qu'on peut dire qu'une femme a maintenant des règles, par la seule raison que sa mère les a eues, comme elle aurait été phthisique peutêtre, si sa mère l'eût été; il y a plus, elle peut être sujette au flux menstruel, même quoique la cause primitive qui introduisit ce besoin ne subsiste plus en elle."—Roussel ("Système de la Femme," p. 134).

Id. . . . "Il y a eu des auteurs qui ne voulaient pas considérer la menstruation comme une fonction inhérente à la nature de la femme, mais comme une fonction acquise, continuant par l'habitude."—Raciborski ("Traité de la Menstruation," p. 17).

Id. . . . "The 'set' of mind, as Professor Tyndall well calls it, whether, as he says, 'impressed upon the molecules of the brain,' or conveyed in any other way, is quite as much a human as an animal phenomenon. Perhaps the greater part of those qualities which we call the characteristics of race are nothing else but the 'set' of the minds of men transmitted from generation to generation, stronger and more marked when the deeds are repeated, weaker and fainter as they fall into disuse. . . . Tyndall says: 'No mother can wash or suckle her baby without having a "set" towards washing and suckling impressed upon the molecules of her brain, and this set, according to the laws of hereditary transmission, is passed on to her daughter. Not only, therefore, does the woman at the present day suffer deflection from intellectual pursuits through her proper motherly instincts, but inherited proclivities act upon her mind like a multiplying galvanometer, to augment indefinitely the amount of the deflection. *Tendency* is immanent even in spinsters, to warp them from intellect to baby-love.' (Essay: "Odds and Ends of Alpine Life.") Thus, if we could, by preaching our pet ideal, or in any other way induce one generation of women to turn to a new pursuit, we should have accomplished a step towards bending all future womanhood in the same direction."—Frances Power Cobbe (Essay: "The Final Cause of Woman").

See also Note XXVI., 7.

6.—" *e'en the virgin*

An experienced gynæcologist writes:—"For want of proper information in this matter, many a frightened girl has resorted to every conceivable device to check what she supposed to be an unnatural and dangerous hæmorrhage, and thereby inaugurated menstrual derangements which have prematurely terminated her life, or enfeebled her womanhood. I have been consulted by women of all ages, who frankly attributed their physical infirmities to the fact of their having applied ice, or made other cold applications locally, in their frantic endeavours to arrest the first menstrual flow."

What general practitioner has not met with analogous instances in the circle of his own patients?

7.— . . . *ere fit* . . .

"The physician, whose duty is not only to heal the sick, but also to prevent disease and to improve the race, and hence who must be a teacher of men and women, should teach sound doctrine in regard to the injurious results of precocious marriage. Mothers especially ought to be taught, though some have learned the lesson by their own sad experience, that puberty and nubility are not equivalent terms, but stand for periods of life usually separated by some years; the one indicates capability, the other fitness, for reproduction."—Parvin ("Obstetrics," p. 91).

Id. . . . "The *general maturity of the whole frame* is the true indication that the individual, whether male or female, has reached a fit age to reproduce the species. It is not one small and unimportant symptom by which this question must be judged. Many things go to make up virility in man; the beard, the male voice, the change in figure, and the change in disposition; and in girls there is a long period of development in the bust, in the hips, in bone and muscle, changes which take years for their proper accomplishment before the girl can be said to have grown into a woman. All this is not as a rule completed before the age of twenty. Woman's form is not well developed before she is twenty years old; her pelvis, which has been called the laboratory of generation, has not its perfect shape until then; hence an earlier maternity is not desirable. If the demand is made on the system before that, the process of development is necessarily interfered with, and both mother and offspring suffer. Even in countries where the age of marriage is between twenty and twenty-five, where, therefore, the mother has not been weakened by early maternity, it is remarked that the strongest children are born to parents of middle age, *i.e.*, from thirty-five to forty; this, the prime of life to the parent, is the happiest moment for the advent of her progeny."—Mrs. Pechey Phipson, M.D. (Address to the Hindoos).

See also end of Note XXIV., 1.

8.—"*Abnormal fruits of birth*

Dr. John Thorburn, in his "Lecture introductory to the Summer Course on Obstetric Medicine," Victoria University, Manchester, 1884, says:—"Let me briefly remind you of what occurs at each menstrual period. During nearly one week out of every four there occurs the characteristic phenomenon of menstruation, which in itself has some temporary *impoverishing effect*, though, in health, nature speedily provides the means of recuperation. Along with this we have a marked disturbance in the circulation of the pelvis, leading to alterations in the weight, conformation, and position of the *uterus*. We have also tissue changes occurring, ***not perhaps yet thoroughly understood***, but leading to ruptures in the ovary, and to exfoliation of the uterine lining membrane, *a kind of modified abortion, in fact.*

These changes in most instances are accompanied by signs of pain and discomfort, which, if they were not periodic and physiological, would be considered as symptoms of disease."

(The italics are not in the original.) Here is certainly cogent evidence of "abnormal fruit of birth," and the learned doctor seems to be on the verge of making the involuntary discovery. But he follows the usual professional attempt (see Note XXX., 4) to class menstruation as a physiological and not a pathological fact; as a natural, painful incident, and not an acquired painful consequence. His half-declared argument, that, because an epoch of pain is periodic it is therefore not symptomatic of disease, is a theory as unsatisfactory as novel.

Id. Some of the facts connected with parthenogenesis, alternate generation, the impregnation of insects, &c., passed on through more than one generation, would show by analogy this class of phenomena not extranatural or unprecedented, but abnormal and capable of rectification or reduction to pristine normality or non-existence. The fact of occasional instances of absence of menstruation, yet with a perfect potentiality of child-bearing, indicates this latter possibility. That the male being did not correspondingly suffer in personal physiological sequence is explicable on the ground that the masculine bodily function of parentage cannot be subjected to equal forced sexual abuse; though in the male sex also there is indication that excess may leave hereditary functional trace. And that, again, a somewhat analogous physical abnormality may be induced by man in other animals, compare the intelligent words of George Eliot in her poem, "A Minor Prophet":—

" . . . milkmaids who drew milk from cows,
With udders kept abnormal for that end."

In confirmation of which see "Report of the Committee, consisting of Mr. E. Bidwell, Professor Boyd Dawkins, and others, appointed for the purpose of preparing a Report on the Herds of Wild Cattle in Chartley Park, and other parks in Great Britain." The Committee state, concerning a herd of wild cattle at Somerford Park, near Congleton, of which herd "the cows are all regularly milked," that "The udders of the cows here are as large as in ordinary domestic cows, which is not the case in the herds which are not milked."—("Report of the British Association," 1887, p. 141.)

XXIV.

1.—"*Misread by man*

"You say 'We marry our girls when they reach puberty,' and you take as indication of that stage one only, and that the least certain, of the many changes which go to make up maturity. It is the least certain because the most variable, and dependent more upon climate and conditions of life than upon any true physical development. No one would deny that a strong country girl of thirteen was more mature physically than a girl of eleven brought up in the close, unwholesome atmosphere of a crowded city, yet you say the latter has attained to puberty, and that the former has not. Into such discrepancies has this physiological error led you.

Without going into the domain of physiology for proof of assertion, let me draw your attention to the very practical proof of its truth, which you have in the fact well-known to you all, that girls married at this so-called period of puberty do not, as a rule, bear children till some years later, *i.e.*, till they really approach maturity. I allow that you share this error with all but modern physiologists. Even if marriage is delayed till fourteen, where conception takes place immediately, sterility follows after; but where the girl is strong and healthy there is a lapse of three or four years before child-bearing begins, a proof that puberty had not been reached till then, although menstruation had been all the time existent. Of course there are exceptional cases, but does not the consensus of experience point to these as general truths?"—Mrs. Pechey Phipson, M.D. (Address to Hindoos).

Id. " . . . *sign of his misdeed.*"

See Note XXVI., 6.

4.— . . . *victim to his adult rage.*"

Of this, as existent to the present age, abundant direct and collateral evidence is given by a *brochure* entitled "A Practical View of the Age of Consent Act, for the benefit of the Mahomedan community in general, by the Committee of the Mahomedan Literary Society of Calcutta," published by that Society, in June, 1891, as "an accurate exposition of the object and scope of the new law, in the clearest possible language, for the benefit of the Mahomedans, particularly the ignorant classes, and circulated widely in the vernacular languages for that purpose."

The following are extracts from the pamphlet :—

Par. 1. "Now that the Age of Consent Act has been passed by his Excellency the Viceroy, in Council, and as there is every likelihood of its provisions not being sufficiently well understood by the Mahomedan community in general, and by the ignorant Mahomedans in particular, owing to the use of technical legal phraseology in the drafting of the Act, it seems to the Committee of Management of the Mahomedan Literary Society of Calcutta, to be highly desirable that the object and intention of the Government in passing this Act, as well as its scope and the manner in which it is to be administered by the Criminal Authorities, should be laid down on paper in the clearest and easiest language possible, for the information and instruction of the Mahomedan population, and particularly of such of them as are not conversant with legal technicalities."

Par. 2. "The Committee are of opinion that such a course will be highly beneficial to members of their community, inasmuch as it will show to them distinctly what action on the part of a Mahomedan husband towards his young wife has been made, by the recent legislation, a heinous criminal offence of no less enormity than the offence of *rape*, and punishable with the same heavy punishment."

Par. 3. "It is hoped that they will thereby be put on their guard against committing, or allowing the commission of an act which *they have hitherto been accustomed to think lawful and innocent*, but which has now been made into a heinous offence. . "

Par. 9. " . . . There has already been a provision in the Indian Penal Code, passed more than thirty years ago, that a man having sexual intercourse with his own wife, with or without her consent, she *being under the age of ten years*, shall be considered guilty of the offence of *rape*, and shall be liable to transportation for life, or to rigorous or simple imprisonment for ten years."

Par. 10. "From this it follows that, under the Penal Code a man having sexual intercourse with his own wife, with or without her consent, if she is *above ten* years of age, shall not be considered to have committed the offence of *rape*. But the Act that has just been passed, in amendment of the above provision in the Penal Code, *raises* the age of consent from *ten* to *twelve* years, and provides that a man having sexual intercourse with his own wife, even with her consent, shall be considered to be guilty of the offence of rape, if the wife be of any age under *twelve completed years*. This is all the change that has been made in the law."

Par. 11. "It having been ascertained, from various sources, that in some parts of the country husbands cohabit with their wives before they have attained to the age of *twelve* years, and even before they have arrived at *puberty*, the result of such intercourse being in many cases to cause injury to the health, and even danger to the life of the girls, and to generate internal maladies which make them miserable throughout their lives, and such a state of things having come to the notice of Government, they have considered it their duty to put a stop to it, and this is the object of the present legislation."

Par. 12. "The law does not interfere with the age at which a girl may be married, but simply prohibits sexual intercourse with her by her husband before she is *twelve* years of age."

Par. 13. "It is therefore *incumbent* upon all husbands and their guardians (if they are very young and inexperienced lads) to be very careful that sexual intercourse does not take place until the girl-wife has *passed* the age of *twelve* years. It will also be the duty of the guardians of the girl-wife not to allow her husband to cohabit with her until she has attained that age.'

Par. 17. "   The Mahomedan law (*i.e.*, religious law) distinctly sanctions consummation of marriage *only* when the wife has reached puberty, and has besides attained such physical development as renders her fit for sexual intercourse, and it is *not imperative* upon a Mahomedan husband to consummate marriage with his wife when she is *under* the age of *twelve* years. Even in those rare cases in which the wife attains to puberty and the necessary physical development before the age of *twelve*, a Mahomedan husband *may*, without infringing any canon of the Mahommedan Ecclesiastical Law, *abstain* from consummating his marriage with her *until* she attains that age.

Par. 18. "The above will clearly show that the Act recently

passed by the Legislature does not, in any way, interfere with the Mahomedan religion, and *no* Mahomedan husband will be considered to have committed a *sin* if he abstains from consummating marriage with his wife *before* she is *twelve* years of age."

(The pamphlet is published, as aforesaid, by the Mahomedan Literary Society of Calcutta, of which the patron is the Hon. Sir Charles A. Elliott, K.C.S.I., C.I.E., and the president Prince Mirza Jahan Kadar Bahadur (of the Oudh family), and is signed by the secretary, Nawab Abdool Luteef Bahadur, C.I.E.; Calcutta, 16 Taltollah, 22nd June, 1891.)

The italics, as above, exist in the original (with the exception of those in Par. 3), and serve, singularly enough, to point for us a moral very much deeper than that intended. It is a happy fact that British feeling, supported by the growing sentiment of the more intelligent and educated of the native population, has effected even so slight an amelioration of law and custom, and we may hope for and press forward to further improvement. Though the utterance quoted above is only that of the Mahomedan section, it is, of course, understood that the law does not apply or point to them alone, but to all the peoples and sects of India; and that the approval of this legislation is also general among the enlightened of those other creeds. (See end of Note XVII., 8.)

Singular confirmatory evidence as to the distressing prevalence of this child-marriage is incidentally given in the following paragraph from the *Times* of 31st March, 1892:—

"A correspondent of the *Times of India* mentions some odd

instances of minor difficulties which have occurred in the working of the amended Factory Act, which came into force in India at the commencement of the present year. The limit of age for 'full-timers' in factories is fixed at fourteen years, and as very few native operatives know their children's ages, or even their own, the medical officer has, in passing lads and girls for work, to judge the age as best he can—generally, as in the case of horses, by examining their teeth. If he concludes that they are under fourteen, he reduces them to 'half-timers.' In one Bombay mill recently a number of girls were thus sent back as under age who were actually mothers, and several boys who were fathers were also reduced ; and one of the latter was the father, it is said, of three children. The case of these lads is particularly hard, for, with a wife and child, or perhaps children, to support, life, on the pay of a 'half-timer,' must be a terrible struggle."

Lest it should be objected that such abuses—with their consequences—as have been instanced in India, are peculiar to that country or civilisation, and that their discussion has therefore no bearing on our practices in England, and the physical consequences ensuant here, it will be salutary to recall what has been our own national conduct in this matter of enforcement of immature physical relations on girl children or "wives" within times of by no means distant date. Blackstone tells in his "Commentaries," Book II., Chap. VIII., that "The wife must be above nine years old at her husband's death, otherwise she shall not be endowed, though in Bracton's time the age was indefinite, and dower was then only due 'si uxor possit dotem promereri, *et virum sustinere.*'" Whereupon Ed. Christian makes the following note, worthy of the most careful meditation :—"Lord Coke informs us that 'if the wife be past the age of nine years at the time of her husband's death, she shall be endowed, of what age soever her husband be, albeit he were but *four* years old. Quia junior non potest dotem promereri, *et virum sustinere.*' (Coke on Litt., 33.) This we are told by that grave and reverend judge without any remark of surprise or reprobation. But it confirms the observation of Montesquieu in the 'Spirit of Laws,' Book XXVI., Chap. III. 'There has been,' says he, 'much talk of a law in England which permitted girls seven years old to choose a husband. This law was shocking two ways; it had no regard to the time when Nature gives maturity to the understanding, nor to the time when she gives maturity to the body.' It is abundantly clear, both from our law and history, that formerly such early marriages were contracted as in the present times are neither attempted nor thought of.

"This was probably owing to the right which the lord possessed of putting up to sale the marriage of his infant tenant. He no doubt took the first opportunity of prostituting (*i.e.*, selling in marriage) the infant to his own interest, without any regard to age or inclinations. And thus what was so frequently practised und permitted by the law would cease even in other instances to be considered with abhorrence. *If the marriage of a female was delayed till she was sixteen, this benefit was entirely lost to the lord her guardian.*

"Even the 18 Eliz., cap. 7, which makes it a capital crime to abuse a consenting female child under the age of ten years, seems to leave an exception for these marriages by declaring only the *carnal and unlawful* knowledge of such woman-child to be a felony. Hence the abolition of the feudal wardships and marriage at the Restoration may perhaps have contributed not less to the improvement of the morals than of the liberty of the people."—(Blackstone's Comm., Christian's Edition, 1830, Vol. II., p. 131.)

6.— . . . *manner* "

"Manner," or "custom" is the early Biblical definition for this habit (*vide* Gen. xviii. 11, and xxxi. 35). It may be noticed that the word is not rendered or translated as "nature." It is also called "sickness" (Lev. xx. 18); and "pollution" (Ezek. xxii. 10). See also Note XXV. 8.

The authorised version of the Bible is here referred to. The euphemisms attempted in the recent revised version as amendments of some of these passages are equally consonant with the argument of this note.

XXV.

1.—" *Vicarious punishment* . "

Revolting was the shock to the writer, coming, some years ago, with unprejudiced and ingenuous mind, to the study of the so-called "Diseases of Women," on finding that nearly the whole of these special "diseases," including menstruation, were due, directly or collaterally, to one form or other of *masculine* excess or abuse. Here is a nearly coincident opinion, afterwards met with:—"The diseases peculiar to women are so many, of so frequent occurrence, and of such severity, that half the time of the medical profession is devoted to their care, and more than half its revenues depend upon them. We have libraries of books upon them, special professorships in our medical colleges, and hosts of doctors who give them their exclusive attention. . . . The books and professors are all at fault. They have no knowledge of the causes or nature of these diseases" (or at least they do not publish it, or act on it), "and no idea of their proper treatment. Women are everywhere outraged and abused. When the full chapter of woman's wrongs and sufferings is written, the world will be horrified at the hideous spectacle. . . . "—T. L. Nichols, M.D. ("Esoteric Anthropology," p. 198).

So, again, in speaking of menorrhagia:—"The causes of this disease, whatever they are, must be removed. Thousands of women are consigned to premature graves; some by the morbid excesses of their own passions, but far more by the sensual and selfish indulgences of those who claim the legal right to murder them in this manner, whom no law of homicide can reach, and upon whose victims no coroner holds an inquest."—(*Op. cit.*, p. 301.)

2.— . . . *grievous toll* . . ."

And this in every grade of society, even to the pecuniary loss, as well as discomfort, of the labouring classes of women.

"Statistics of sickness in the Post Office show that women" (these are unmarried women) "are away from their work more days than men."—(Sidney Webb, at British Association, 1891.)

5.—" *no honest claim.*"

The *Times* of Aug. 3, 1892, reports a paper by Professor Lombroso, of Turin (at the International Congress of Psychology, London), in which occurs the following:—"It must be observed that woman was exposed to more pains than man, because man imposed submission and often even slavery upon her. As a girl, she had to undergo the tyranny of her brothers, and the cruel preferences accorded by parents to their male children. Woman was the slave of her husband, and still more of social prejudices. Let them not forget the physical disadvantage under which she had to labour. She might justly call herself the pariah of the human family."

The word is apt and corroborative, for it was no honest act—it was not Nature, but human cruelty and injustice that formed a pariah.

8.—' . . . *opprobrious theme.*"

Conf. ancient and mediæval superstitions and accusations on the subject. Raciborski notes these aspersions (Traité, p. 13):—"Pline prétendait que les femmes étant au moment des règles pouvaient dessécher les arbres par de simples attouchements, faire périr des fruits, &c., &c." And a further writer says more fully:—"Pliny informs us that 'the presence of a menstrual woman turns wine sour, causes trees to shed their fruit, parches up their young fruit, and makes them for ever barren, dims the splendour of mirrors and the polish of ivory, turns the edge of sharpened iron, converts brass into rust, and is the cause of canine rabies. In Isaiah xxx. 22, the writer speaks of the defilement of graven images, which shall be cast away as a menstruous cloth; and in Ezekiel xviii. 6, and xxxvi. 17, allusions of the same import are made." Unless we accept the antiquated notion of a "special curse" on women, how reconcile the idea of an "ordinance of Nature" being so repulsively and opprobriously alluded to? Well may it be said:—"Ingratitude is a hateful vice. Not only the defects, but even the illnesses which have their source in the excessive" (man-caused) "susceptibility of woman, are often made by men an endless subject of false accusations and pitiless reproaches."—(M. le Docteur Cerise, in his Introduction to Roussel, p. 34.)

XXVI.

1.—"*Thoughts like to these are breathings of the truth.*"

"I submit that there is a spiritual, a poetic, and, for aught we know, a spontaneous and uncaused element in the human mind, which ever and anon suddenly, and without warning, gives us a glimpse and a forecast of the future, and urges us to seize truth, as it were, by anticipation. In attacking the fortress we may sometimes storm the citadel without stopping to sap the outworks. That great discoveries have been made in this way the history of our knowledge decisively proves."—H. T. Buckle ("Influence of Women on the Progress of Knowledge").

Id. . . "Then there is the inner consciousness—the psyche—that has never yet been brought to bear upon life and its questions. Besides which, there is a supersensuous reason. Observation is perhaps more powerful an organon than either experiment or empiricism. If the eye is always watching, and the mind on the alert, ultimately chance supplies the solution."—Jefferies ("The Story of My Heart," Chap. X.).

Id. . . "Women only want hints, finger-boards, and finding these, will follow them to Nature. The quick-glancing intellect will gather up, as it moves over the ground, the almost invisible ends and threads of thought, so that a single volume may convey to the mind of woman truths which man would require to have elaborated in four or six." — Eliza W. Farnham ("Woman and Her Era," Vol. II., p. 420).

3.—" *futile mannish pleas* "

Roussel details fully some nine of these main theories or explanations of the habitude. ("Système," Note A.)

6.—" *In blindness born* . .

"Tous ces faits nous induisent fortement à conjecturer qu'il a dû exister un temps ou les femmes n'étaient point assujettiés à ce tribut incommode; que le flux menstruel bien loin d'être une institution naturelle, est au contraire un besoin factice contracté dans l'état sociale."—Roussel (*Op. cit.*, Chap. II.).

Note that menstruation (scriptural "sickness") remains a pathological incident, not, as childbirth, an indubitably natural and normal physical function.

See also Note XXX., 4.

Id.—" . . . *in error fostered*

Not only the habit itself, but its causes. And this by medical, *i.e.*, assumedly curative, practitioners. As to which "fostering," medical and clinical manuals afford abundant spontaneous and ingenuous testimony, and also of other professional practices of instigation, or condonation, or complicity, at which a future age will look aghast. *Conf.* the following from Whitehead, "On the Causes and Treatment of Abortion and Sterility" (Churchill, 1847):—

"In a case under my care of pregnancy in a woman, with *extreme deformity of the pelvis*, wherein it was considered advisable to *procure abortion* in the fifth month of the process, the ergot alone was employed, and, at first, with the desired effect." [The italics are not in the doctor's book; he remarks nothing wrong or immoral, and—in an unprofessional person—illegal, and open to severest penalty; he is simply detailing the effects of a specified medicament.] "It was given in *three successive* pregnancies, and in each instance labour pains came on after eight or ten doses had been administered, and expulsion was effected by the end of the third day. It was perseveringly tried in a fourth pregnancy in the same individual, and failed completely" (p. 254).

There is an ominous silence as to whether the patient's health or life also "failed completely."

See further a case noted on p. 264, *op. cit.* :—

1st child, still-born, in eighth month, April 1832.
2nd „ abortion at end of 6th month.
3rd „ „ „ 6th month.
4th „ „ „ 5th month.
5th „ „ soon after quickening, Summer, 1838.
6th „ still born, 7th October, 1839.
7th „ no clear record given.

Also other somewhat parallel cases given, the constant incidental accompaniment being painful physical suffering and grave inconvenience, frequently with fatal results. Medical records are full of similar histories. To the unsophisticated mind, two questions sternly suggest themselves: Firstly, Is it meet or right for an honourable profession, or any individual member of it, to be *particeps criminis* in such proceedings as the above? and, secondly, is the indicated connubial morality on any higher level, or likely to be attended with any better consequences, than the prior ignorant or savage abuses which are responsible for woman's present physical condition?

The advocacy of cardinal reform in this direction—in the wrong done both to the individual and the race—is urgent part of the duty of our newly-taught medical women. Nor are their eyes closed nor their mouths dumb in the matter. Dr. Caroline B. Winslow is quoted by the *Woman's Journal* of Boston, U.S, 16th Jan., 1892, as saying in an article on "The Right to be Well Born": "What higher motive can a man have in life than to labour steadily to prepare the way for the coming of a higher, better humanity? . . . Dense ignorance prevails in our profession, and is reflected by laymen. All their scientific studies and years of medical practice have failed to convict men of the wrongs and outrages done to women; wrongs that no divine laws sanction, and no legal enactments can avert.

"The physician is a witness of the modern death-struggles and horrors of maternity; he sees lives pass out of his sight; he makes vain attempts to restore broken constitutions, broken by violating divine laws that govern organic matter: laws that are obeyed by all animal instinct; yet all this knowledge, observation, and experience have failed to reveal to the benighted intellect and obtuse moral sense of the ordinary practitioner this great wrong. He makes no note of the unhallowed abuse that only man dares; neither will he mark the disastrous and deteriorating effect of this waste of vital force on his own offspring. The mental, moral, and physical imperfections of the rising generation are largely the result of outraged motherhood."

7.—" *The spurious function growing*

Mr. Francis Darwin, in a paper on "Growth Curvatures in Plants," says of the biologist, Sachs, who had made researches in the same phenomena: "He speaks, too, of *custom* or *use*, *building up* the specialised 'instinct' for certain curvatures. (Sachs' 'Arbeiten,' 1879.) These are expressions consistent with our present views."—(Presidential Address to the Biological Section of the British Association, 1891.)

In the same section was also read a paper by Francis Darwin and Dorothea F. N. Pertz, "On the *Artificial* Production of Rhythm in Plants," in which were detailed results very apposite to this "growing of a spurious function."

8.— . . *almost natural use the morbid mode appears.*"

"So true is it that unnatural generally only means uncustomary, and that everything which is usual appears natural."—J. S. Mill ("The Subjection of Women," p. 22).

XXVII.

1.—" *Grievous the hurt*

Buckle notes one of the many incidental evil results in his "Common Place Book," Art. 2133:—

"It has been remarked that in our climate women are

more frequently affected with insanity than men, and it has been considered very unfavourable to recovery if they should be worse at the time of menstruation, or have their catamenia in very small or immoderate quantities." (Paris and Fonblanque's "Medical Jurisprudence," Vol. I., p. 327).

5.—" . . . *reintegrate in frame and mind.*"

"Thus then you have first to mould her physical frame, and then, as the strength she gains will permit you, to fill and temper her mind with all knowledge and thoughts which tend to confirm its natural instincts of justice, and refine its natural tact of love."—John Ruskin ("Of Queens' Gardens," p. 154).

XXVIII.

5, 6.—" . . *given in our hand,*
Is power the evil hazard to command."

"That which is thoughtlessly credited to a non-existent intelligence should really be claimed and exercised by the human race. It is ourselves who should direct our affairs, protecting ourselves from pain, assisting ourselves, succouring and rendering our lives happy. We must do for ourselves what superstition has hitherto supposed an intelligence to do for us. These things speak with a voice of thunder. From every human being whose body has been racked with pain; from every human being who has suffered from accident or disease; from every human being drowned, burned, or slain by negligence, there goes up a continually increasing cry louder than the thunder. An awe-inspiring cry dread to listen to, against which ears are stopped by the wax of superstition and the wax of criminal selfishness. These miseries are your doing, because you have mind and thought and could have prevented them. You can prevent them in the future. You do not even try."—R. Jefferies ("The Story of My Heart," pp. 149 *et seq.*).

Id "From one philosophical point of view, that of Du Prel, the experiments are already regarded as proving that the soul is an organising as well as a thinking power. Bernheim saw an apoplectic paralysis rapidly improved by suggestion. . . . The more easily an idea can be established in the subject, the quicker a therapeutic result can be induced. . . . I think that hardly any of the newest discoveries are so important to the art of healing, apart from surgery, as the study of suggestion. . . . Now that it has been proved that even organic changes can be caused by suggestion, we are obliged to ascribe a much greater importance to mental influences than we have hitherto done."—Dr. Albert Moll ("Hypnotism," pp. 122, 318, 320, 325, 327).

Id. . . . "It would, I fancy, have fared but ill with one who, standing where I now stand, in what was then a thickly-peopled and fashionable part of London, should have broached to our ancestors the doctrine which I now propound to you—that all their hypotheses were alike wrong; that the plague was no more, in their sense, Divine judgment, than the fire was the work of any political, or of any religious, sect; but that they were themselves the authors of both plague and fire, and that they must look to themselves to prevent the recurrence of calamities, to all appearance so peculiarly beyond the reach of human control. We, in later times, have learned somewhat of Nature, and partly obey her. Because of this partial improvement of our natural knowledge and of that fractional obedience, we have no plague; because that knowledge is still very imperfect and that obedience yet incomplete, typhus is our companion and cholera our visitor. But it is not presumptuous to express the belief that, when our knowledge is more complete and our obedience the expression of our knowledge, London will count her centuries of freedom from typhus and cholera as she now gratefully reckons her two hundred years of ignorance of that plague which swooped upon her thrice in the first half of the seventeenth century."—T. H. Huxley ("On Improving Natural Knowledge").

And the pestilent malady from which woman specially still suffers is as definitely the result of man's ignorant or thoughtless misdoing, and is as indubitably amenable to rectification, as the plague of the bye-gone ages, or the typhus and cholera of the present.

8.— . . . *pain both prompts and points escape.*"

"All evil is associated more or less closely with pain . . and pain of every kind is so repugnant to the human organism, that it is no sooner felt than an effort is made to escape from it. . . . Alongside of the evolution of evil there has ever been a tendency towards the *elimination* of evil. . The highest intellectual powers of the greatest men have for their ultimate object the mitigation of evil, and the final elimination of it from the earth."—Richard Bithell ("The Creed of a Modern Agnostic," p. 103).

XXIX.

1.—" *woman shall her own redemption gain.*"

In the greatest depth of their meaning remain true the words of Olive Schreiner · "He who stands by the side of woman cannot help her; she must help herself."

Id. . "Nothing is clearer than that woman must lead her own revolution; not alone because it is hers, and that no other being can therefore have her interest in its achievement, but because it is for a life whose highest needs and rights—those to be redressed in its success—lie above the level of man's experiences or comprehension. Only woman is sufficient to state woman's claims and vindicate them."—Eliza W. Farnham ("Woman," Vol. I., p. 308).

(See also Notes to XLVI. 7 and LVIII. 1.)

2.—"*Instructed by the sting of bootless pain.*"

"Toutes les fonctions du corps humain, sauf l'enfantement, sont autant de plaisirs. Dès que la douleur surgit, la nature est violée. La douleur est d'origine humaine. Un corps malade ou a violé les lois de la nature, ou bien souffre de la violation de la loi d'un de ses semblables. La douleur par elle-même est donc le meilleur diagnostic pour le médecin. . . . Entre la loi de la nature et la violation de cette loi, il n'y a que désordres, douleurs et ruines. . La maladie ne vient pas de la nature, elle n'y est même pas. Elle n'est que la violation d'une des lois de la nature. Dès qu'une de ces lois est violée, la douleur arrive et vous dit qu'une loi vient d'être enfreinte. S'il est temps encore, le mal peut être amoindri, expulsé, chassé. . . . La maladie n'est donc que le résultat de la violation d'une loi naturelle. . . La science et la mécanique du corps humain, c'est l'art de vivre d'après les lois de la nature, c'est la certitude que pas un médecin ne possède contre la violation d'une de ces lois un remède autre que d'y rentrer le plus tôt possible. . . . Chaque fois que l'homme s'efforcera de suivre la loi de la nature, il chassera devant soi une centaine de maladies."—Dr. Alexandre Weill ("Lois et Mystères de l'Amour," pp. 41, 91, 24, 85, 83).

3, 4.—"*With Nature ever helpful to retrieve*
The injury we heedlessly achieve."

"Thus, if we could, by preaching our pet ideal, or in any other way induce one generation of women to turn to a new pursuit, we should have accomplished a step towards bending all future womanhood in the same direction."—Frances Power Cobbe (Essay: "The Final Cause of Woman").

See also Note XXIII., 4.

6.—"*Already guerdon rich in hope is shown.*"

"He (Mr. Frederic Harrison) says—'All women, with few exceptions, are subject to functional interruption absolutely incompatible with the highest forms of continuous pressure.' This assertion I venture most emphatically to deny. The actual period of child-birth apart, the ordinarily healthy woman is as fit for work every day of her life as the ordinarily healthy man. Fresh air, exercise, suitable clothing and nourishing food, added to the habitual temperance of women in eating and drinking, have brought about a marvellously good result in improving their average health."—Mrs. Fawcett (*Fortnightly Review*, Nov. 1891).

(See also Note LX., 8.)

8.—" *The sage physician, she*

Not only "sage" physician, but "brave" physician; for brave indeed has been the part she has had to bear against male professional prejudice and jealousy, opposition from masculine vested interests, virulent abuse and even personal violence. So recently as 1888, Dr. Sophia Jex-Blake has to report concerning the medical education of women, that:—

"The first difficulty lies in some remaining jealousy and ill-will towards medical women on the part of a section (constantly diminishing, as I believe) of the medical profession itself. Some twenty years ago the professional prejudice was so deep and so widely spread that it constituted a very formidable obstacle, but it has been steadily melting away before the logic of facts; and now is, with a few exceptions, rarely to be found among the leaders of the profession, nor indeed among the great majority of the rank and file, as far as can be judged by the personal experience of medical women themselves. Unfortunately, it seems strongest just where it has least justification, viz., among the practitioners who devote themselves chiefly to midwifery, and to the special diseases of women. The Obstetrical Society is, so far as I know, still of the same mind as when, in 1874, they excluded Dr. Elizabeth Garrett Anderson, a distinguished M.D. of Paris, from their membership; and the Soho Square Hospital for Women has never revoked its curt refusal to allow me to enter its doors, when, in 1878, I proposed to take advantage of the invitation issued in its report to all practitioners who were specially interested in the cases for which the hospital is reserved. Sometimes this jealousy takes a sufficiently comic form. For instance, I received for two successive years a lithographed circular inviting me by name to send to the *Lancet* the reports of interesting cases that might occur in my dispensary practice, but when I wrote in response to this supposed offer of professional fellowship, I received by next post a hurried assurance from the editor that it was all a mistake, and that, in fact, the *Lancet* could not stoop to record medical experiences, however interesting, if they occurred in the practice of the inferior sex! Probably it will not require many more years to make this sort of thing ridiculous, even in the eyes of those who are now capable of such puerilities.

"The second obstacle lies in the continued exclusion of women from the majority of our Universities, and from the English Colleges of Physicians and Surgeons. Here also the matter may be left to the growth of public opinion as regards those existing bodies which do not depend upon the public purse; but it is time that Parliament should refuse supplies to those bodies whose sense of justice cannot be otherwise awakened, and it is certainly the duty of Government to see that no new charter is granted without absolute security for equal justice to students of both sexes."—Sophia Jex-Blake, M.D. (*Nineteenth Century*, Nov., 1887).

See also Note LVII., 1, and LVIII., 1.

Id. . Progress is indeed being made, surely, yet slowly, for Mrs. Fawcett has still necessity to reiterate, four years afterwards:—

"Make her a doctor, put her through the mental discipline and the physical toil of the profession; charge her, as doctors are so often charged, with the health of mind and body of scores of patients, she remains womanly to her finger tips, and a good doctor in proportion as the truly womanly qualities in her are strongly developed. Poor women are very quick to find this out as patients. Not only from the immediate neighbourhood of the New Hospital for Women, where all the staff are women doctors, but also from the far East of London do they come, because 'the ladies,' as they call them, are ladies, and show their poor patients womanly sympathy, gentleness, and patience, womanly insight and thoughtfulness in little things, and consideration for their home troubles and necessities. It is not too much to say that a woman can never hope to be a good doctor unless she is truly and really a womanly woman. And much the same thing may be said with regard to fields of activity not yet open to women."—Mrs. Fawcett (*Fortnightly Review*, Nov., 1891).

Id. " . . . *saviour of her sex*."

Bebel says:—"Women doctors would be the greatest blessing to their own sex. The fact that women must place themselves in the hands of men in cases of illness or of the physical disturbances connected with their sexual functions frequently prevents their seeking medical help in time. This gives rise to numerous evils, not only for women, but also for men. Every doctor complains of this reserve on the part of women, which sometimes becomes almost criminal, and of their dislike to speak freely of their ailments, even after they have made up their minds to consult a doctor. This is perfectly natural, the only irrational thing about it is the refusal of men, and especially of doctors, to recognise how legitimate the study of medicine is for women." ("Woman," Walther's translation, p. 131.)

Id. . . "As I am alluding to my own experience in this matter, I may perhaps be allowed to say how often in the same place I have been struck with the *contingent* advantages attendant on the medical care by women of women; how often I have seen cases connected with stories of shame or sorrow to which a woman's hand could far more fittingly minister, and where sisterly help and counsel could give far more appropriate succour than could be expected from the average young medical man, however good his intentions. Perhaps we shall find the solution of some of our saddest social problems, when educated and pure-minded women are brought more constantly in contact with their sinning and suffering sisters, in other relations as well as those of missionary effort."—Dr. Sophia Jex-Blake (Essay: "Medicine as a Profession for Women").

XXX.

1.—"*With purer phase* "

A noted specialist in this matter, Dr. Tilt, "basing his conclusions on his own unpublished observations, and on those already made public by M. Brierre de Boismont and Dr. Rawn," has declared what is indeed a generally accepted proposition, that "luxurious living and habits render menstruation precarious, while this function is retarded by out-door labour and less sophisticated habits." ("Proceedings of British Association," 1850, p. 135; "On the Causes which Advance or Retard the Appearance of First Menstruation in Women," by E. J. Tilt, M.D., &c., &c.)

4.—". . . *weakness* . . ."

It is to be carefully kept in mind that this "weakness" (Scriptural, "sickness," Lev. xx., 18) is strictly a pathological incident; while maternity is truly a physiological one; the male false physicists seem in their mental and clinical attitude to have aimed to precisely reverse this definition. (See also Note XXIII., 8, and XXVI., 6.)

5,6.—To the fact related in these two lines there is testimony in nearly every book connected with the subject; and doubtless numerous instances never come to light, owing to the very natural reticence pointed out in Note XXIX., 8. The improved condition reported by Mrs. Fawcett (Note XXIX., 6) is hence more readily verified by women practitioners; and the writer has had detailed personal experiences of perfect health and maternity being co-existent with little or no appearance of the menses in the case of women whose names, if published, would be indubitable guarantee for their accuracy and veracity.

7.—"*Not to neglectful man to greatly care* "

The Report of the British Association for 1850, in summarising the paper above referred to (Note 1), says of Dr. Tilt that, "in discussing what he calls the intrinsic causes which have been supposed to influence menstruation, his observations are rather of a suggestive character, for he considers such causes highly problematical and requiring further investigation." Dr. Tilt rightly emphasises the question as "a matter equally interesting to the physician, the philosopher, and the statesman; and it behoves them to know that this epoch (of menstruation) varies under the influence of causes which for the most part have been insufficiently studied." But the negligence or carelessness reprobated in the verse has again supervened.

Buckle says, concerning this same paper of Dr. Tilt's: "We take shame to ourselves for not having sooner noticed this very interesting and in some respects very important work; the author unknown," (?) "and yet the book has gone through two editions, though written on a subject ignorantly supposed to be going on well. That women can be satisfied with their state shows thair deterioration. That they can be satisfied with knowing nothing, &c." (*sic.*) ("Miscellaneous and Posthumous Works," Vol. I., p. 381.)

The whole passage seems somewhat incoherent, and is unfinished as above, as if left by Mr. Buckle for further consideration. The last two remarks as to women are certainly not written with his usual justice; when we remember how assiduously men have striven to prevent woman's pursuit of physiological knowledge, especially as applied to her own person, it is manifest that the blame for woman's ignorance, or her presumed "satisfaction" therewith, is more fittingly to be reproached to man than to her.

XXXI.

1.—"*Her intellect alert* .

"*Intellectus prelucit voluntati.*"—"Intellect carries the light before the will."—Cardinal Manning (*Review of Reviews*, Vol. V., p. 135).

5, 6.—" . . . *body still is supple unto mind,*
By dint of soul is fleshly form inclined."

Reflecting Plato's teaching, our second worthy Elizabethan poet has said :—

"Every spirit as it is most pure,
And hath in it the more of heavenly light,
So it the fairer body doth procure
To habit in.
For of the Soul the Body form doth take·
For Soul is form, and doth the Body make."

And in our own day, Charles Kingsley says, in serious sportiveness: "The one true doctrine of this wonderful fairy tale is, that your soul makes your body, just as a snail makes its shell." And again: "You must know and believe that people's souls make their bodies just as a snail makes its shell. . . . I am not joking, my little man; I am in serious, solemn earnest."—("The Water Babies," Chaps. III. and IV.

And Elizabeth Barrett Browning ("Aurora Leigh," Book III.)—

" . . . the soul
Which grows within a child makes the child grow."

The physiologists and psychologists, as is not unusual, tardily follow in the wake of the poets. At the International Congress of Experimental Psychology, London, 1892, "Professor Delbœuf said that at all times the mind of man had been capable of influencing the body, but it was only in recent times that this action had been scientifically put in evidence."—(*Times*, August 3rd, 1892.)

And Dr. Albert Moll, of Berlin, had written the year previously, that—"When the practical importance of mental influences becomes more generally recognised, physicians will be obliged to acknowledge that psychology is as important as physiology. Psychology and psychical therapeutics will be the basis of a rational treatment of neuroses. The other methods must group themselves around this; it will be the centre, and no longer a sort of Cinderella of science, which now admits only the influence of the body on the mind, and not that of the mind on the body."—("Hypnotism," p. 328.) See also Note XXVIII., 5.

XXXII.

2.— . . . *woo the absent curse."*

Even Raciborski condemns this common error of treatment:—" . . . quand les jeunes filles de cette catégorie paraissent souffrantes, quel que soit le caractère des souffrances, on est disposé à les attribuer au défaut du flux menstruel, on le regrette, on l'invoque, et l'on tente tout pour le provoquer. Ces idées sont aujourd'hui encore très profondement enracinées dans le public, et sont souvent la cause des entraves au traitement rationnel proposé par les médecins."—(Traité, &c., ed. 1868, p. 377.)

And Mrs. E. B. Duffey very sensibly says:—

"Nature . . . is very easily perverted: and the girl who begins by imagining she is ill or ought to be at such times will end by being really so." ("No Sex in Education," Philadelphia, 1874, p. 79.)

3.—" . . . *counter effort*

"Forel and many others mention that there are certain popular methods of slightly retarding menstruation. In one town many of the young women tie something round their little finger if they wish to delay menstruation for a few days in order to go to a ball, &c. The method is generally effectual, but when faith ceases, the effect also ceases."—Dr. Albert Moll ("Hypnotism," p. 226).

Before quitting this special subject it may be well to remark that little more than the fringe is here indicated of an enormous mass of evidence which affords more than presumptive confirmation and support for the position here taken in the whole question of this "abnormal habit."

4.—" . . . *custom* . . ."—See Note XXIV., 6.

XXXIII.

2.— . . . *newer vigour to the brain.*"

"It is well-known that every organ of the body and, therefore, also the brain, requires for its full development and, consequently, for the development of its complete capability of performance, exercise and persistent effort. That this is and has been the case for thousands of years in a far less degree in woman than in man, in consequence of her defective training and education, will be denied by no one." So says the learned biologist Büchner.—("Man," Dallas's translation, p. 206.)

And Bebel also declares:—"The brain must be regularly used and correspondingly nourished, like any other organ, if its faculties are to be fully developed."—("Woman," Walther's translation, p. 124.)

Dr. Emanuel Bonavia, in the course of an able reply to a somewhat shallow recent disquisition by Sir James Crichton Browne, says:—

"From various sources we have learnt that the brain

tissue, like every other tissue, will *grow* by exercise, and diminish, or degenerate and atrophy by disuse. Keep your right arm tied up in a sling for a month, and you will then be convinced how much it has lost by disuse. Then anatomists might perhaps be able to say—Lo! and behold! the muscles of your right arm have a less specific gravity than those of your left arm; that the nerves and blood-vessels going to those muscles are smaller, and that, *therefore*, the right arm cannot be the equal of the left, and must have a different function!

"Any medical student knows that if you tie the main trunk of an artery, a branch of it will in due course acquire the *calibre* of the main trunk. If, for some reason, it cannot do so, the tissues, which the main trunk originally supplied, *must* suffer, and be weakened, from want of a sufficient supply of blood. Man, and especially British man, has evolved into what he is by endless trouble and struggle through past ages. He has had to develop his present brain from very small beginnings. It would, therefore, now be the height of folly to allow the thinking lobes of the mothers of the race to revert, intellectually, by disuse step by step again to that of the lower animals, from which we all come. That of course many may not believe, but it may be asked, how can he or she believe these things with such weakened lobes, as he or she may have inherited from his or her mother? How indeed! If there is anything in nature that is true, it is this—That if you don't use your limbs they will atrophy; if you don't use your eyes they will atrophy; if you don't use your brain it will atrophy. They all follow the same inexorable law. Use increases and sharpens ; disuse decreases and dulls. Diminished size of the frontal lobes and of the arteries that feed them mean nothing if they do not mean that woman's main thinking organ, that of the intellect, is, as Sir James would hint, degenerating by *disuse* and neglect."—("Woman's Frontal Lobes," *Provincial Medical Journal*, July, 1892.)

These facts suggest strongly that the waste at present induced in the female body by the menstrual habit might well be absorbed in increase of brain power; and indeed, that this evolved habit has hitherto persistently sequestrated and carried off from woman's organism the blood force that should have gone to form brain power. This explanation would dispose of the awkwardly imagined "plethora" theory, as well as one or two others, of sundry gynæcologists.

And the converse—that the increased appropriation of the blood in forming brain power induces a state of bodily well-being, free from the present waste and weariness,—would certainly seem to be borne out by such evidence as that of the Hon. John W. Mitchell, the president of the Southern California College of Law, who said in a recent lecture:—

"Not only in this, but in other countries, there are successful women practitioners (of Law), and in France, where the preparatory course is most arduous, and the term of study longest, a woman recently took the highest rank over 500 men in her graduating examinations, and during the whole six years of class study she only lost one day from her work." (See Note LVII., 1.)

A few words may here be said as to the dubitable

question of the relative size of the brain in man and woman, though the matter may not be of great import, from more than .one reason. For, as Bebel observes : "Altogether the investigations on the subject are too recent and too few in number to allow of any definite conclusions" (p. 123). A. Dumas fils says ("Les Femmes qui Tuent," p. 196)—"Les philosophes vous démontreront que, si la force musculaire de l'homme est plus grande que celle de la femme, la force nerveuse de la femme est plus grande que celle de l'homme; que, si l'intelligence tient, comme on l'affirme aujourd'hui, au développement et au poids de la matière cérébrale, l'intelligence de la femme pourrait être declarée supérieure à celle de l'homme, le plus grand cerveau et le plus lourd comme poids, étant un cerveau de femme lequel pesait 2,200 grammes, c'est a dire 400 grammes de plus que celui de Cuvier. On ne dit pas, il est vrai, que cette femme ait écrit l'équivalent du livre de Cuvier sur les fossiles."

To which last remark may be replied, again in the words of Bebel,—"Darwin is perfectly right in saying that a list of the most distinguished women in poetry, painting, sculpture, music, science, and philosophy, will bear no comparison with a similar list of the most distinguished men. But surely this need not surprise us. It would be surprising if it were not so. Dr. Dodel-Port (in "Die neuere Schöpfungsgeschichte") answers to the point, when he maintains that the relative achievements would be very different after men and women had received the same education and the same training in art and science during a certain number of generations."—("Woman," p. 125.)

"It is of small value to say—yes, but look how *many* men excel and how few women do so. True, but see how much repression men have exercised to *prevent* women from even equalling them, and how much shallowness of mind they have encouraged. All manner of obstructions, coupled with ridicule, have been put in their way, and until women succeed in emancipating themselves, most men will probably continue to do so, simply because they have the power to do it. When women become emancipated, that is, are placed on social equality with men, this senseless, mischievous opposition will die a natural death."—E. Bonavia, M.D. ("Woman's Frontal Lobes").

To revert to the question of brain weight, one of the first of English specialists says:—

"Data might, therefore, be considered to show, in the strongest manner, how comparatively unimportant is mere bulk or weight of brain in reference to the degree of intelligence of its owner, when considered as it often is, apart from the much more important question of the relative amount of its grey matter, as well as of the amount and perfection of the minute internal development of the organ either actual or possible."—Dr. H. C. Bastian ("The Brain as an Organ of Mind," p. 375.)

The American physiologist Helen H. Gardener states:—

"The differences (in brain) between individuals of the same sex—in adults at least, are known to be much more marked than any that are known to exist between the sexes. Take the brains of the two poets Byron and Dante. Byron's weighed 1,807 grammes, while Dante's weighed only 1,320 grammes, a difference of 487 grammes. Or take two statesmen, Cromwell and Gambetta. Cromwell's brain weighed 2,210 grammes, which, by the way, is the greatest healthy brain on record; although Cuvier's is usually quoted as the largest, a part of the weight of his was due to disease, and if a diseased or abnormal brain is to be taken as the standard, then the greatest on record is that of a negro criminal idiot; while Gambetta's was only 1,241 grammes, a difference of 969 grammes. Surely it will not be held because of this that Gambetta and Dante should have been denied the educational and other advantages which were the natural right of Byron and Cromwell. Yet it is upon this very ground, by this very system of reasoning, that it is proposed to deny women equal advantages and opportunities, although the difference in brain weight between man and woman is said to be only 100 grammes, and even this does not allow for difference in body weight, and is based upon a system of averages, which is neither complete nor accurate."—(Report of the International Council of Women, Washington, 1888, p. 378.)

Concerning an assertion that "the specific gravity of both the white and grey matter of the brain is greater in man than in woman," Helen H. Gardener says:—"Of this point this is what the leading brain anatomist in America (Dr. E. C. Spitzka) wrote: 'The only article recognised by the profession as important and of recent date, which takes this theory as a working basis, is by Morselli, and he is compelled to make the sinister admission, while asserting that the specific gravity is less in the female, that with old age and with insanity the specific gravity increases.' If this is the case I do not know that women need sigh over their shortcoming in the item of specific gravity. There appear to be two very simple methods open to them by which they may emulate their brothers in the matter of specific gravity, if they so desire. One of these is certain, if they live long enough; and the other—well, there is no protective tariff on insanity."—(*Loc. cit.*, p. 379.)

Helen Gardener further appositely observes:—"The brain of no remarkable woman has ever been examined. Woman is ticketed to fit the hospital subjects and tramps, the unfortunates whose brains fall into the hands of the profession as it were by mere accident, while man is represented by the brains of the Cromwells, Cuviers, Byrons, and Spurzheims. By this method the average of men's brains is carried to its highest level in the matter of weight and texture; while that of women is kept at its lowest, and even then there is only claimed 100 grammes' difference!" —(*Loc. cit.*, p. 380.)

And she concludes her exhaustive paper with the closing paragraph of a letter to herself from Dr. E. C. Spitzka, the celebrated New York brain specialist:—"You may hold me responsible for the following declaration: That any statement to the effect that an observer can tell by looking at a brain, or examining it microscopically, whether it belonged to a female or a male subject, is not founded on carefully-observed facts. . . . No such difference has ever been demonstrated, nor do I think it will be by more elaborate methods than we now possess. Numerous female brains exceed numerous male brains in absolute weight, in complexity of convolutions, and in what brain anatomists would call the nobler proportions. So that he who takes these as his criteria of the male brain may be grievously mistaken in attempting to assert the sex of a brain dogmatically. If I had one hundred female brains and one hundred male brains together, I should select the one hundred containing the largest and best-developed brains as probably containing fewer female brains than the remaining one hundred. More than this no cautious experienced brain anatomist would venture to declare."—(*Loc. cit.*, p. 381.)

Charles Darwin has clearly summarised this question of comparison of brain:—"No one, I presume, doubts that the large size of the brain in man, relatively to his body, in comparison with that of the gorilla or orang, is closely connected with his higher mental powers. . . . On the other hand, no one supposes that the intellect of any two animals or of any two men can be accurately gauged by the cubic contents of their skulls. It is certain that there may be extraordinary mental activity with an extremely small absolute mass of nervous matter; thus the wonderfully diversified instincts, mental powers, and affections of ants are generally known, yet their cerebral ganglia are not so large as the quarter of a small pin's head. Under this latter point of view the brain of an ant is one of the most marvellous atoms of matter in the world, perhaps more marvellous than the brain of man."—("The Descent of Man," Chap. IV.)

3.—"*Wide shall she roam* . ."

John Ruskin says, of training a girl:—"Let her loose in the library, I say, as you do a fawn in a field. It knows the bad weeds twenty times better than you, and the good ones too; and will eat some bitter and prickly ones, good for it, which you had not the slightest thought were good." —("Sesame and Lilies," p. 167.)

6.— . . . *murmurings* . . "

"Man thinks that his wife belongs to him like his domesticated animals, and he keeps her therefore in slavery. There are few, however, who wear their shackles without feeling their weight, and not a few who resent it. Madame Roland says: 'Quand vous parlez en maître, vous faites penser aussitôt qu'on peut vous résister, et faire plus peutêtre, tel fort que vous soyez. L'invulnerable Achille ne l'était pas partout.'"—Alexander Walker, M.D. ("Woman as to Mind, &c.," p. 353).

"Why do women not discover, when 'in the noon of beauty's power,' that they are treated like queens only to be deluded by hollow respect, till they are led to resign, or not assume, their natural prerogatives? Confined then in cages like the feathered race, they have nothing to do but to plume themselves and stalk with mock majesty from perch to perch. It is true they are provided with food and raiment, for which they neither toil nor spin, but health liberty, and virtue are given in exchange."—Mary Wollstonecraft ("Vindication of the Rights of Woman," Chap. IV.). See also Note XL., 5.

"What have they (men) hitherto offered us in marriage, with a great show of generosity and a flourish of trumpets, but the dregs of a life, and the leavings of a dozen other women? Experience has at last taught us what to expect and how to meet them."—Lady Violet Greville (*National Review*, May, 1892).

See also Note XX., 2.

8.—" *Lest that her soul should rise*

" Laboulaye distinctly advises his readers to keep women in a state of moderate ignorance, for 'notre empire est détruit, si l'homme est reconnu' (Our empire is at an end when man is found out)."—(Note to Bebel, Walther's translation, p. 73.)

Id.—" . *break his time-worn yoke.*"

As already shown, the subjugation of woman has not been an incident of Western "civilisation" alone. Mrs. Eliza W. Farnham relates that "When a Chinese Mandarin in California was told that the women of America were nearly all taught to read and write, and that a majority of them were able to keep books for their husbands, if they chose to do so, he shook his head thoughtfully, and, with a foreboding sigh, replied, 'If he readee, writee, by'n-by he lickee all the men.' Was that a barbarian sentiment, or rather, perhaps, a presentiment of the higher sovereignty coming?"—("Woman and Her Era," Vol. II., p. 41.)

XXXIV.

5.— . . . *his servitude*

" Villeins were not protected by Magna Charta. "*Nullus liber homo capiatur vel imprisonetur*,' &c., was cautiously expressed to exclude the poor villein, for, as Lord Coke tells us, the lord may beat his villein, and, if it be without cause, he cannot have any remedy. What a degraded condition for a being endued with reason!"—Edward Christian ("Note to Blackstone's Commentaries," Book II., Chap. VI.).

Mr. Christian's exclamation of concern is doubtless meant to apply to the serf, yet was not the lord's position equally despicable?

6.—" . *in turn was master to a slave.*"

This was, in fact, simply extending the spirit of the feudal system (with its serfdom as just pictured) a little further. Buckle exemplifies in ancient French society the servility descending from one grade to another in man:—"By virtue of which each class exercising great power over the one below it, the subordination and subserviency of the whole were completely maintained. . . . This, indeed, is but part of the old scheme to create distinctions for which Nature has given no warrant, to substitute a superiority which is conventional for that which is real, and thus try to raise little minds above the level of great ones. The utter failure, and, as society advances, the eventual cessation of all such attempts is certain." But, meanwhile, evil accompaniments are apparent, as Buckle further instances by saying: "Le Vassor, who wrote late in the reign of Louis XIV., bitterly says: 'Les Français accoutumés à l'esclavage, ne sentent plus la pesanteur de leurs chaînes.'"—("History of Civilisation in England," Vol. II., Chaps III., IV.)

That the foregoing habits or foibles are human rather

than simply masculine, or that the imitation of them very naturally spreads to the other sex, would seem to be shown by such evidence as Letourneau gives :—

"In primitive countries the married woman—that is to say, the woman belonging to a man—has herself the conscience of being a thing, a property (it is proved to her often and severely enough), but she does not think of retaliating, especially in what concerns the conjugal relations. Moreover, as her condition is oftenest that of a slave overburdened with work, not only does she not resent the introduction of other women in the house of the master, but she desires it, for the work will be so much the less for herself. Thus among the Zulus the wife first purchased strives and works with ardour in the hope of furnishing her husband with means to acquire a second wife, a companion in misery over whom, by right of seniority, she will have the upper hand."—("The Evolution of Marriage," Chap. VIII.)

Yet, in point of fact, this is not woman seeking to establish her own dominion, but rather to secure somewhat more of freedom for herself. As Alexandre Dumas fils tells us, concerning the Mormon women :—

"Non seulement elles donnent leur consentement à leurs maris, quand ils le leur demandent pour un nouveau mariage, mais elles sont quelquefois les premières à leur proposer une nouvelle femme qui a, disent-elles, des qualités nécessaires à la communauté, en réalité pour augmenter un peu la possession d'elles-mêmes, c'est-à-dire leur liberté."—("Les Femmes qui Tuent," &c., p. 169.)

8.—" *vassalage to man.*"

The Laureate Rowe makes his heroine bitterly but with reason exclaim :—

"How hard is the condition of our sex,
Through every state of life the slaves of man!
In all the dear delightful days of youth,
A rigid father dictates to our wills,
And deals out pleasure with a scanty hand:
To his, the tyrant husband's reign succeeds;
Proud with opinions of superior reason,
He holds domestic business and devotion
All we are capable to know, and shuts us,
Like cloistered idiots, from the world's acquaintance
And all the joys of freedom. Wherefore are we
Born with high souls, but to assert ourselves,
Shake off this vile obedience they exact,
And claim an equal empire o'er the world?"
—("The Fair Penitent," Act III. sc. 1.)

Letourneau shows the state of feminine tutelage carried still further: "We shall find that in many civilisations relatively advanced, widowhood even does not gratify the woman with a liberty of which she is never thought worthy." And later on he quotes from the code of Manu, Book V.:— "A little girl, a young woman, and an old woman ought never to do anything of their own will, even in their own house. During her childhood a woman depends on her father; during her youth on her husband; her husband being dead, on her sons; if she has no sons, on the near relatives of her husband; or in default of them, on those of her father; if she has no paternal relatives, on the

Sovereign. A woman ought never to have her own way."—("The Evolution of Marriage," Chaps. VII., XII.)

Can a man be esteemed a human or even a rational being, who would accept or tolerate such terms for the life of his sister woman—the mother of the generations to come?

See also Note XVII., 8.

XXXV.

1, 2.—" *fearing that the slave herself might guess*
The knavery of her forced enchainedness."

"Here I believe is the clue to the feeling of those men who have a real antipathy to the equal freedom of women. I believe they are afraid, not lest women should be unwilling to marry . . . but lest they should insist that marriage should be on equal conditions; but all women of spirit and capacity should prefer doing almost anything else, not in their own eyes degrading, rather than marry, when marrying is giving themselves a master, and a master too of all their earthly possessions. And truly, if this consequence were necessarily incident to marriage, I think that the apprehension would be very well founded."—J S. Mill ("The Subjection of Women," p. 51).

See also Note XL., 4.

5.— . . . *dogmas* . . . .

These dogmas which, under the guise of religion, were imposed on the acceptance of womanhood, may be aptly summarised and epitomised in the following lines from one of the hierarchs of the system :—

"To whom thus Eve, with perfect beauty adorn'd :
'My author and disposer, what thou bidd'st
Unargued I obey : so God ordains ;
God is thy law, thou mine ; to know no more
Is woman's happiest knowledge, and her praise.'"
—("Paradise Lost," Book IV., 634.)

Concerning which words of Milton well may Mary Wollstonecraft observe, with a quiet sarcasm :—"If it be allowed that women were destined by Providence to acquire human virtues, and, by the exercise of their understandings, that stability of character which is the firmest ground to rest our future hopes upon, they must be permitted to turn to the fountain of light, and not forced to shape their course by the twinkling of a satellite."—("Vindication of the Rights of Woman," Chap. II.)

Milton also discoursed learnedly, but self-interestedly, concerning divorce, claiming for the husband a privilege and option which he utterly denied to the wife :—" the power and arbitrement of divorce from the master of the family, into whose hands God and the law of all nations had put it . . . that right which God from the beginning had entrusted to the husband."—("The Doctrine and Discipline of Divorce.")

It was this same mediæval moralist who trained his daughters in the pronunciation of various languages, that they might minister to his comfort by reading to him in those tongues ; while he carefully withheld from them any knowledge of the meaning of the words they were uttering. Could a greater insult or a more degrading office be inflicted on a cultured human intellect? Small wonder that his daughters were sufficiently "undutiful and unkind"—as Milton styled it—to leave him some years before his death. That the possessor of the same virile intellect which penned the "Areopagitica," with its brave freedom, could tolerate and promulgate the servitude and degradation of one half of humanity indicates in him a mental darkness as gross and as pitiable as his physical blindness.

6, 7.—" . . . *sanctimonious name*
Of 'woman's duty' "

"Hitherto the world has been governed by brute force only, which means that the stronger animal, man, has kept the weaker in subjection, allowing her to live only in so far as she ministered to his comforts; that he has not unnaturally made laws and fixed customs to suit his own pleasure and convenience, always at the expense of the woman; and, what is worse, that he has in all countries given a religious sanction to his vices, in order to bend the woman to his wishes. . . . I might also add that all cruel customs relating to woman have been imposed upon her under the guise of religion, and hence, though so injurious and baneful to herself, she is even slower to change them than the man. There is hardly any cruel wrong which has been inflicted in the course of ages by man upon his fellow-man that has not been justified by an appeal to religion."—Mrs. Pechey Phipson, M.D. ("Address to the Hindoos of Bombay").

Id. . . . "There is nothing which men so easily learn as this self-worship: all privileged persons, and all privileged classes, have had it. . . Philosophy and religion, instead of keeping it in check, are generally suborned to defend it."—J. S. Mill ("The Subjection of Women," p. 77).

Id. . . . A. Dumas fils speaks of "les femmes, ces éternelles mineures des religions et des codes;" and of "les arguments à l'aide desquels l'Eglise veut mettre les femmes de son côté"; and shows as the effect that "Il y a des femmes honnêtes, esclaves du devoir, pieuses. Leur religion leur a enseigné le sacrifice. Non seulement elles ne se plaignent pas des épreuves à traverser mais elles les appellent pour mériter encore plus la récompense promise, et elles les bénissent quand elles viennent. Tout arrive, pour elles, par la volonté de Dieu, et tout est comme il doit être dans cette vallée des larmes, chemin de l'éternité bienheureuse. . . . D'ailleurs elles ne lisent ni les journaux, ni les livres où il est question de ces choses-là; cette lecture leur est interdite. Si, par hasard, elles avaient connaissance de pareilles idées, elles en rougiraient, elles en souffriraient pour leur sexe, et elles prieraient pour celles qui se laissent aller à propager de si dangereuses erreurs et à donner de si deplorables exemples. . . . Mais, pas plus que le bonheur, la ruse, l'ignorance, la misère et la servitude, la foi aveugle, l'extase, et l'immobilité volontaire de l'esprit ne sont des arguments sans réplique."—("Les Femmes qui Tuent," &c., pp. 10, 91, 103.)

The evil which Dumas points out is common to all

religions, of whatever race or make; the hall-mark of every creed, from Confucianism to Comtism, has been the subjection of woman, under the affectation of advocating her highest interests. The pious compound has usually been altered to meet the growing intellectual requirements of common-sense and justice and humanity, and hence the precepts of religion as to feminine conduct have by no means always lain in such lines as the multitude in our modern Western civilisation still enjoins on women. No more than the whole and universal attitude of religion, ancient or modern, as regards woman, is exposed or expressed in the following recapitulation of present or historic facts:—"It is not the chastity of women, as we understand it, but her subjection, that Japanese morality requires. The woman is a thing possessed, and her immorality consists simply in disposing freely of herself.

"As regards prostitution, Brahmanic India is scarcely more scrupulous than Japan, and there again we find religious prostitution practised in the temples, analogous to that which in ancient Greece was practised at Cyprus, Corinth, Miletus, Tenedos, Lesbos, Abydos, &c. (Lecky, 'History of European Morals,' Vol. I., p. 103). According to the legend, the Buddha himself, Sakyamouni, when visiting the famous Indian town of Vasali, was received there by the great mistress of the courtesans. (Mrs. Spier, 'Life in Ancient India,' p. 28)."—Letourneau ("The Evolution of Marriage," Chap. X.).

The enforcement, or commendation, or acceptance of the practice of prostitution, with its profanation of the dignity and individuality of woman, and its utter carelessness and disregard for either her physical or intellectual well-being, is indubitable evidence of the man-made (*i.e.*, male) origin of such a scheme of religion or ethics or economics. For, as Mrs. Eliza W. Farnham truly remarks:—"If a doubt yet remains on the mind of any reader that I have stated truly the part of the masculine as cause in this terrible phenomenon, let it be considered how man has always introduced prostitution in every country that he has visited, and every island of the sea. Does anyone believe, for example, that if the voyages of discovery and trade had been made by women instead of men, to the islands of the Pacific, this scourge would have been left as the testimony of their visit, so that, in a few generations, the populations native there would have fallen a literal sacrifice to their sensuality, as they are actually falling to man's at this day? There is no comment needed on the illustration, I am sure. The common sense of every reader will furnish the best comment and answer the question correctly."—("Woman and Her Era," Vol. II., p. 299.)

Id. . . . Lastly, but most convincingly, as to the wilful and intentional degradation and subjugation of woman by the teaching and rites of religion, let it be noted that, among the Jews, the very fact of being a woman is made a disgrace; and woman, the mother of the human race, is insulted accordingly. In the morning synagogue service of prayer, directly after unitedly blessing "Adonai," for bestowing on the barn-door fowl the power to distinguish between night and day, and for not having created the worshippers present heathens or slaves, each member of the male portion of the congregation thanks the same

Adonai "that Thou hast not fashioned me as a woman," while each member of the segregated female portion of the company is instructed to submissively give thanks "that Thou hast fashioned me after Thine own pleasure." The male thanks for not being heathens seem, under the circumstances, conspicuously premature.—(See "Ohel Jakob," *i.e.*, "Jacob's Temple," the "Daily Prayer of the Israelites," Fraenkel's ed., Berlin.)

That the spirit of this Mosaic or Hebrew sexual teaching, with its incongruous assertions and inferences, has communicated itself deeply to Christianity, may be observed from such passages as 1 Tim. ii. 13, 14; 1 Cor. vii., 9; Eph. v. 24; Col. iii. 18; 1 Pet. iii. 1, 5; and many others.

Id. . . . Buckle quotes from "Fergusson on the Epistles," 1656, p. 242:—"The great and main duty which a wife, as a wife, ought to learn, and so learn as to practice it, is to be subject to her own husband." (See also Note XVII., 8.) And Buckle further cites, from "Fox's Journal," "After the middle of the seventeenth century the Quakers set up 'women's' meetings, to the disgust of many, and (query, because) in the teeth of St. Paul's opinion."—("Miscellaneous and Posthumous Works," Vol. I., pp. 375, 384.)

Id . . . As already said, the "sanctimonious" claim of "woman's duty" runs through all religions. Here, for instance, is what is reported in a leader of the *Manchester Guardian* of August 15th, 1892:—

"In this country no one would place suicide in the ranks of the virtues. Here it is a crime, but in China under certain circumstances it is regarded as an act of heroism and devotion worthy of sympathy and of national recognition. Thus the Governor of Shansi forwarded to the Emperor of China a memorial setting forth the virtues as daughter and wife of a lady in that province. She was of good family, both her father and grandfather having been officials in the district. At the age of ten she showed her love for her mother in a peculiarly Chinese fashion. One of the Celestial beliefs is that medicine acquires efficacy by having mingled with it some human flesh, and the little girl cut some from her own body to be used for the purpose of curing an illness which threatened her mother's life. In 1890 she was married to an 'expectant magistrate,' whose expectations were realised by his appointment last autumn to a judicial post. What she had, as a good daughter, done for her mother, she, as a good wife, did also for her husband, who fell ill; but her remedy was inefficacious, and he died. She was now in a position which, according to the Chinese code of ethics, has no responsibilities for a woman. Without parents, husband, or children to demand her affectionate care, she decided to commit suicide, and apparently not only communicated her intentions to those around her, but had their sympathy and support in her decision. We are told that, 'only waiting till she had completed the arrangements for her husband's interment, she swallowed gold and powder of lead. She handed her *trousseau* to her relations to defray her funeral expenses, and made presents to the younger members of the family and the servants, after which, draped in her state robes, she sat waiting her end. The poison began to work, and soon all was over." The story of a distracted wife seeking refuge in death from the sorrows of widowhood might doubtless be told of any country in Europe, but the sequel is possible only in China. The Governor of Shansi, struck with the courage of the lady in what he evidently regards as a very proper though somewhat unusual exhibition of conjugal affection, asks in his memorial that the virtuous life and death of the lady may be duly commemorated. The prayer of the memorial has been granted by the Emperor and a memorial arch is to be erected in honour of the sucide.

8.—" *this reasoned day* . . "

See Note XVII., 8.

XXXVI.

1.—" *By cant condoned* .

"Much has been said by Guizot on the influence of women in developing European civilisation. It is at least certain that several of the fathers did everything they could to diminish that influence. Tertullian bitterly complains of the insolence of women who venture to teach and to baptise. He allows that in case of necessity baptism may be administered by a layman, but never by a woman. Again, among the other crimes of the heretics he particularly enumerates the insolence of their women, who ventured to teach, to dispute, &c., &c. In 'De Cult. Faem,' lib. I. Cap. I., he says: 'Let women remember that they are of the sex of Eve, who ruined mankind, and let them therefore repair this ignominy by living rather in dust than in splendour.'"—Buckle ("Common-Place Book," Note 1870).

Id.—" *man fashioned woman's 'sphere.'* "

"We deny the right of any portion of the species to decide for another portion, or any individual for another individual, what is, and what is not, 'their proper sphere.' The proper sphere for all human beings is the largest and highest which they are able to attain to. What this is, cannot be ascertained without complete liberty of choice."—Mrs. Harriet Mill ("Enfranchisement of Women," *Westminster Review*, July 1851).

6.—" . *civil law* . ."

For example of this let us look at the law of our own

country in even recent times. Blackstone says: "The husband (by the old law) might give his wife moderate correction. . . . But this power of correction was confined within reasonable bounds, and the husband was prohibited from using any violence to his wife, *aliter quam ad virum ex causa regiminis et castigationis uxoris suæ licite et rationabiliter pertinet* (*i.e.*, otherwise than to a man for the ruling and punishment of his wife, lawfully and reasonably pertains). The civil law gave the husband the same or a larger authority over his wife, allowing him for some misdemeanours, *flagellis et fustibus acriter verberare uxorem* (*i.e.*, to severely beat his wife with whips and cudgels), for others, only *modicam castigationem adhibere* (to administer a moderate chatisement). But with us, in the politer reign of Charles the Second, this power of correction began to be doubted, and a wife may now (*circ.* 1750) have security of peace against her husband; or in return, a husband against his wife. Yet the lower rank of people, who were always fond of the old common law," (query, were the women fond of it?) "still claim and exert their ancient privilege: and the courts of law will still permit a husband to restrain a wife of her liberty in case of any gross misbehaviour." ("Commentaries," Edward Christian's Ed., Book I., Chap. XV.)

Such was undoubtedly the generally accepted and not infrequently acted upon assumption; and it is certain that the Courts of Law would, in the event of a wife absenting herself from her husband, order her return to his custody; and would, and did imprison her in default of her compliance. And this state of things continued until—as Mrs.

Wolstenholme Elmy records in her history of the celebrated "Clitheroe case"—

"At length, in the year 1891, and, as in the case of the negro Somerset, upon the return to a writ of *habeas corpus*, there have been found judges bold enough and just enough to set aside the ancient saws and maxims, resting mainly upon *obiter dicta* and loose phrases of previous judges used in reference to hypothetical cases never actually before the Courts, and to declare plainly and straightly that the personal slavery of the wife is no part of the law of England. The actual words of the Lord Chancellor in dealing with the return to the writ are, as reported by the *Times*, March 20th, 1891, as follows:—

"After stating the circumstances of the marriage, the decree, and the refusal of the wife to cohabit, it states: 'I therefore took my wife, and have since detained her in my house, using no more force or restraint than necessary to take her and keep her.' That is the return which seeks to justify an admitted imprisonment of this lady. I do not know that I am able to express in sufficiently precise language the difference between 'confinement' and 'imprisonment,' but if there is any distinction, I can only say that upon these facts I should find an imprisonment, and looking at the return it is put as a broad proposition that the right of the husband, where there has been a wilful absenting of herself by the wife from her husband's house—that it is his right to seize possession of his wife by force, and detain her in his house until she renders him conjugal rights. That is the proposition of law involved in the return, and I am not prepared to assent to it. The Legislature has expressly deprived the Matrimonial Court of the power of imprisoning the wife for refusal to comply with a decree for restitution of conjugal rights, and the result of such a system of law, if the husband had the power, would be that whereas the Court had no power to hand the wife over into her husband's hands, but only to punish her for contempt by imprisonment under the control of the Court, and without any circumstances of injury or insult, and even that power was taken away, the husband might himself of his own motion seize and imprison her until she consented to the restitution of conjugal rights. That is the proposition I am called upon to establish by holding this return to be good. *I am of opinion that no such right or power exists in law. I am of opinion that no such right ever did exist in our law.* Whatever authorities may be quoted for any such proposition, it has always been subject to this condition: that where she has a complaint of, or is apprehensive of, ill-usage, the Court will never interfere to compel her to return to her husband's custody. Now this brings me to the particular circumstances of this transaction. I am prepared to say that no English subject has a right to imprison another English subject (who is *sui juris*, and entitled to a judgment of his or her own) without any lawful authority, but if there were any qualification of that proposition I should be of opinion that on the facts of this case it would afford an ample justification to any Court for refusing to allow the husband in this case to retain the custody of his wife.'

"On these and other grounds the Lord Chancellor declared that the return of the writ was bad, and ordered that the lady be restored to her liberty, the other judges concurring."—("The Decision in the Clitheroe Case and its Consequences," pp. 3, 4.)

Lord Esher was one of the two other Judges, both concurring, who formed the Court of Appeal which granted the writ, and a few days subsequently he gave from his place in the House of Lords the following further statement of his judgment and views :—

"As I was a party to the judgment, which seems to have been more misunderstood than any judgment I recollect, I, perhaps, may be excused from making an observation. It was urged before the Court of Appeal that by the law of England a husband may beat his wife with a stick if she refuses to obey him, and that if a wife refused her husband conjugal rights, whatever that phrase may mean, which I have never been able to make out, he may imprison her until she restores him conjugal rights, or satisfies him that she will. All that the Court of Appeal decided was that a husband cannot by the law of England, if the wife objects, lawfully do either of those things. Those intelligent people who have declared that the judgment is wrong must be prepared to maintain the converse—namely, that if a wife disobeys her husband he may lawfully beat her; and if she refuses him a restitution of conjugal rights he may imprison her, it was urged, in the cellar, or in the cupboard, or, if the house is large, in the house, by locking her in it and blocking the windows. I thought, and still think, that the law does not allow these things. . . ."—(The *Times*, 17th April, 1891.)

Mrs. Wolstenholme Elmy further tells us that :—

"To Lord Selborne the married women of this country owe a further debt of gratitude for his introduction n 1884 of the Matrimonial Causes Act of that session, which put an end to the punishment by imprisonment of the husband or wife who refused to obey the decree of the Court for restitution of conjugal rights. The arguments of Mr. Lankester and Mr. Finlay in the Clitheroe case, based upon this abolition of the power of the Court to imprison for disobedience, are known to everyone. It would be destructive not only to personal freedom, but a gross infraction of justice and common-sense, were a husband to be permitted to exercise on his own behalf and at his own pleasure a prerogative of punishment which had been withdrawn from the Court.

"That this power of imprisonment was not a mere *brutum fulmen*, but a terrible reality in former days, may be learned from a Suffolk case, early in the present century. A wife in contempt of court, a lady of good family in Suffolk, was imprisoned in Ipswich goal for disobeying a decree requiring her to render conjugal rights to her husband. At the end of a year and ten months she became in want of the common necessaries of life, and was reduced to the gaol allowance of bread and water; she suffered from rheumatism and other maladies, which were aggravated by the miseries of her imprisonment; and after many years of such suffering died in prison—for she never went back to her husband."—("The Decision in the Clitheroe Case and its Consequences," p. 9.)

But while the law has thus been needfully amended in England, a further evil effect has meantime supervened in our dependency of India; for this faculty of imprisonment by the Courts for non-compliance with their order in the event specified, which has been abolished in England, seems to be still existent and appealed to in our Indian Courts. (See Note XXII., 2.) The strange thing is that the suit for the restitution of conjugal rights is not a matter of native law, but an inadvertent and apparently entirely unintentional introduction from our English system; the very judges who administer the Indian Law being at a loss to account for its appearance in their practice. One authority, in seeking the solution of the problem, declares that—"Mr. —— 'could not find any enactment directly establishing suits for the restitution of conjugal rights, and believed there were none; but that they had been recognised in a Stamp Act, and again in the Limitation of Suits Act passed in 1871.' The material point is that Indian lawgivers have not consciously given this remedy to those who did not possess it before; but that it has slipped into our law without design. Mr. —— thinks 'That this class of suits was known in the old Supreme Courts, in the Presidency towns, and as between Europeans; and it was not an improper subject of legislation as regards Stamp Duty or Limitation by Time: but being spoken of without qualification was held by the High Courts to be available for all classes of the Indian communities.' If this theory be true, it accounts in an easy way for a change effected without any intention of the Rulers at all. It is worth enquiry into under this aspect." Yes, enquiry and rectification hand in hand!

Id.—" *and part divine.*"

The fact has been that male lawgivers, in whatever land, have generally asserted for their code of feminine ethics or conduct a divine origin, and have announced the punishment for breach thereof as a divine injunction. In very few instances, indeed, was there any attempt to decree an equal punishment to the male who was partner with the female in a mutual breach of this morality, and very frequently no punishment of the male attached at all; and even in the few cases where such a punishment was nominally threatened, the man's share in the offence was most generally connived at, and passed unpunished. This double code of morality has a flagrant exemplification in the English Law of Divorce, by which, while a man can procure a Decree of Divorce on the simple ground of the adultery of his wife, a woman cannot obtain a like decree for her husband's adultery unless that offence be accompanied by such treatment of herself as the Court will recognise as "cruelty," or with "desertion." The double scheme of sexual morality, so revoltingly tolerated, in so far as man is concerned, by "society" in the present day is too patent to need further words here. And the repulsive cant is still that, while the man is allowed to go free, the punishment of the woman is due and commendable as in accordance with "divine law." (See Note XIV., 3.)

XXXVII.

3, 4.—" . . . *lowest boor is lordly 'baron' styled,*
And highest bride as common 'feme' reviled."

" husband and wife; or, as most of our elder law books call them, 'baron' and 'feme.'"—(Blackstone's "Commentaries," Bk. I. Chap. 15.)

But the context of the words "baron" and "feme" involved something more than a mere *façon de parler* of the law books. Edward Christian says, in Note 23 to the Chapter in "Blackstone" above quoted :—"Husband and wife, in the language of the law, are styled *baron* and *feme ;* the word baron, or lord, attributes to the husband not a very courteous superiority. But we might be inclined to think this merely an unmeaning technical phrase, if we did not recollect, that if the baron kills his feme it is the same as if he had killed a stranger or any other person ; but if the feme kills her baron it is regarded by the laws as a much more atrocious crime, as she not only breaks through the restraints of humanity and conjugal affection, but throws off all subjection to the authority of her husband. And, therefore, the law denominates her crime a species of treason, and condemns her to the same punishment as if she had killed the king. And for every species of treason (though in petit treason the punishment of men was only to be drawn and hanged), till the 30 Geo. III., Chap. 48, the sentence of woman was to be drawn and burnt alive."

And Mr. Courtney Kenny says, on the same point, that the English Law of Marriage in the twelfth century had "clothed the humblest husband with more than the authority of a feudal lord, and merged his wife's legal existence altogether in his own."—("History of the Law of Married Women's Property," p. 8.)

And he exemplifies the position of the "feme" as being accurately depicted in the words of Petruchio :—

"I will be master of what is mine own,
She is my goods, my chattels ; she is my house,

My household stuff, my field, my barn,
My horse, my ox, my ass, my anything."
—("The Taming of the Shrew," Act III., scene 2.)

The picture of the past masculine proprietorship and "bullyism" is scarcely overdrawn. Ere a distant day Englishmen will shudder in reflecting on the male creatures who were their progenitors.

5, 6.—" *The tardier fear that grants the clown a share*
In his own governance, denies it her."

By a leading article on Woman Suffrage, in the *Times* of 29th April, 1892, a clear light is thrown on the causes which largely influenced the extension of the Parliamentary franchise to the poorer class of male citizens,—"a share of political power which they are not particularly well fitted to use," says the *Times* ;—and which denied the same right of franchise to women of whatever class. The intellect of the *Times* enounces that—

"Without desiring to disparage the sex in any way, we must venture to maintain that in both camps a large female contingent would be a mischievous element. The female Conservative politician would be an obstacle to all rational reform; the female Liberal politician would be the advocate of every crude and febrile innovation. No doubt we have put plausible arguments in the mouths of mere logic-choppers by treating the franchise as a right rather than as a privilege and a trust. Men can demand a share of ***political power which they are not particularly well fitted to use***, because they possess *de facto* a share of the physical force upon which all political arrangements ultimately repose. Women do not possess such physical force, and, therefore, can prefer no such claim."

Passing over, as unworthy of serious refutation, the wild

assertions due to sex-bias in the first part of the above extract, it may be noted how instantly the lauded masculine weapon of logic is discarded and contemned as soon as it points in the direction of equal justice for woman. The "physical force" question is further dealt with in Note XLV., 6. But considering the words we have italicised, does not the whole of the *Times* exposition as above justify the appellation of cowardly "fear"? (See also p. 78.)

Id. . . . Yet an even more unworthy thing than denial of the suffrage has taken place, in that English women have been really robbed of their earlier franchises. A lady Poor Law Guardian of the Tewkesbury Union has written:—

" . . . the present position of women in regard to the various franchises is anomalous and contradictory, unworthy of that great growth of freedom which the nineteenth century has given to men, and degenerate as regards the position which women held in the days of the Plantagenets and the Tudors. Freedom for women has not broadened down 'from precedent to precedent.' Rather has it suffered by unnecessary legislative interference. Every woman, except the Queen, is, politically, non-existent. It was not always so. Restrictions unknown to our ancient constitution have crept in. . . . Chief Justice Lee is reported to have cited a case (in a manuscript collection of Hakewell's), Catherine *v.* Surrey, in which it was expressly decided, that a *feme sole*, if she has a freehold, may vote for members of Parliament; and a further one (from the same collection), Holt *v.* Lyle, in which it was decided, that a *feme sole* householder may claim a voice for Parliament men; but, if married, her husband must vote for her; whilst Justice Page declared, 'I see no disability in a woman from voting for a Parliament man.' So closely, in the minds of our Judges, were the local and Parliamentary franchises bound up, that a question as to the rights of women in local voting seemed to involve considerations as to their right to vote for Parliament men.

"Yet, even in the matter of these local franchises, women have suffered, and do suffer, from legislative tinkering and sex-biassed decisions in our law courts.

"Down to 1835, women, possessing the qualifications which entitled men to vote, voted freely in municipal elections, and in some important cities, such as London and Edinburgh, the civic rights even of married women, possessing a separate qualification from the husband, were well established. The Municipal Corporations Act of 1835, however (passed by the Whig administration of Lord Melbourne), was framed upon the evil precedent of the Reform Act of 1832, and by the use of the words 'male persons,' in treating of the franchises under it, disfranchised every woman in the boroughs to which it applied, and this disfranchisement lasted for thirty-four years.

'Nevertheless, in non-corporate districts, women continued to vote as freely as before, and thus secured the ultimate restitution of the rights of their disfranchised sisters in incorporated districts; for, when in 1869, on the consideration of the Municipal Franchise Bill of that year, these peculiar facts were brought to the notice of the House of Commons, and it was shown that the incorporation of any district involved the summary disfranchisement of the women ratepayers, the House, without a dissentient word, or any shadow of opposition, adopted the proposal to omit the word 'male' before the word 'person' in Section 1 of the Bill, and thus restored the rights of the women ratepayers, of whom many thousands voted, as a consequence of the passing of the Act, in the municipal elections of the following November."—Mrs. Harriett McIlquham ("The Enfranchisement of Women: An Ancient Right, a Modern Need," pp. 5, 12, 13.

8.—" . . . *infants*, *felons*, *fools*

This legal courteousness has afforded Miss Frances Power Cobbe the text for an instructive paper: "Criminals, Idiots, Women, and Minors: Is the Classification Sound?" (*Fraser's Magazine*, December, 1868.)

A recent instance of the official collocation is to be found in the Act 5 and 6 Vict., Cap. 35, Sec. 41:—

"And be it enacted, that the trustee, guardian, tutor, curator, or committee of any person, being an infant, or married woman, lunatic, idiot, or insane, and having the direction, control, or management of the property or concern of such infant, married woman, lunatic, idiot, or insane person, whether such infant, married woman, lunatic, idiot, or insane person shall reside in the United Kingdom or not," etc., etc.

XXXVIII.

7.— . . . *every bond erased*

"In the struggle of the races, keeping in view the teachings of evolutionists, the most reasonable and sensible thing, in addition to its *justness*, appears to be this :

"First, to place women on an equal footing with men, socially, and *in the eyes of the law.* Before *that* is done, it is useless to talk about women's superiority or equality. It is all breath and words, or paper and ink. In the eyes of the law she is man's inferior. That is not all. In the eyes of the law the most cultured woman is inferior to the most uncultured man ; she is, in fact, pretty much on a level with a baby, or a boy or girl under age. Moreover, the most cultured woman in the United Kingdom is considered inferior, politically, to the American negro !

"Second, let the two sexes settle matters among themselves, as far as intellect is concerned, as men now settle matters among themselves, without imposing on each other any disability. Those of both sexes who are weak will soon find their intellectual level ; and those of both sexes who are strong will soon come to the front."—Emanuel Bonavia, M.D. ("Woman's Frontal Lobes").

XXXIX.

2.— . . . *equal power of rule*

"Where women walk in public processions in the streets
the same as the men,
Where they enter the public assembly and take places
the same as the men; . . .
Where the city of the cleanliness of the sexes stands,
Where the city of the healthiest fathers stands,
Where the city of the best bodied mothers stands,
There the great city stands."

—Walt Whitman ("Song of the Broad Axe").

3.—"*Her voice in council and in senate* . . ."

"Is there so great a superfluity of men fit for high duties, that society can afford to reject the service of any competent person? Are we so certain of always finding a man made to our hands for any duty or function of social importance which falls vacant, that we lose nothing by putting a ban on one half of mankind and refusing beforehand to make their faculties available, however distinguished they may be? And even if we could do without them, would it be consistent with justice to refuse to them their fair share of honour and distinction, or to deny to them the equal right of all human beings to choose their occupation (short of injury to others) according to their own preferences, at their own risk? Nor is the injustice confined to them, it is shared by those who are in a position to benefit by their services. To ordain that any kind of persons shall not be physicians, or shall not be advocates, or shall not be members of parliament, is to injure not them only, but all who employ physicians, or advocates, or elect members of parliament."—J. S. Mill ("The Subjection of Women," p. 94).

4.—" . . *harmonising word* . .."

.. the main reason why so many thoughtful women now claim direct Parliamentary representation is an unselfish one. They desire to take their full share in the service of the race; to help to solve those grave social problems now so urgently pressing, and which demand for their solution the combined resources of the wisdom, experience, and heart of both halves of humanity. They know that the time is fast coming—if, indeed, it be not already come—which will need for its direction and control something more than diplomatic cleverness or political manœuvring, which will demand the clearer conscience and the more sensitive perception of justice born of imaginative sympathy. It is because they hope and believe that in virtue of their faculty of motherhood they can contribute somewhat of these elements to the world's well-being, and can thus speed its progress towards a nobler future, that they claim full right and power to follow and fulfil their highest conceptions of duty."—Elizabeth C. Wolstenholme Elmy ("The Decision in the Clitheroe Case and its Consequences," p. 17).

7.—"*Self-reverent each and reverencing each.*"

—A line from Part VII. of Tennyson's "Princess."

Id. . . "The exigencies of the new life are no more exclusive of the virtues of generosity than those of the old, but it no longer entirely depends on them. The main foundations of the moral life of modern times must be justice and prudence; the respect of each for the rights of every other, and the ability of each to take care of himself." —J. S. Mill ("The Subjection of Women," p. 159).

XL.

1.—" . . . *but a slave himself*

"The domination of either sex over the other paralyses the dominion of either."—Ellen Sarah, Lady Bowyer (Letter to *Daily News*, 24th October, 1891).

Id.

"Can man be free if woman be a slave?
Chain one who lives, and breathes this boundless air
To the corruption of a closed grave!
Can they whose mates are beasts, condemned to bear
Scorn, heavier far than toil or anguish, dare
To trample their oppressors?"
—Shelley ("The Revolt of Islam," Canto 2, s. xliii.).

2.—". . . *she to shape her own career be free* . "

"Not less wrong—perhaps even more foolishly wrong—is the idea that woman is only the shadow and attendant image of her lord, owing him a thoughtless and servile obedience, and supported altogether in her weakness by the pre-eminence of his fortitude. This, I say, is the most foolish of all errors, respecting her who was made to be the helpmate of man. As if he could be helped effectively by a shadow, or worthily by a slave."—John Ruskin ("Of Queens' Gardens," p. 125).

4.—"*Free mistress of her person's sacred plan.*"

Eliza W. Farnham (in "Woman and Her Era," Vol. II., p. 92) clearly enunciates the depth of degradation and slavery from which woman's person must be freed:—"When this mastery is established, and ownership of her becomes a fixed fact, she who was worshipped, vowed to as an idol, deferred to as a mistress, required to conform herself to nothing except the very pleasant requirement that she should take her own way in everything; to come and go, to accept or reject, to do or not, at her own supreme pleasure—this being may find herself awaking in a state of subjection which deprives her of the most sacred right to her own person—makes her the slave of an exacting demand that ignores the conditions, emotions, susceptibilities, pains, and pleasures of her life, as tyrannically and systematically as if she were indeed an insensate chattel."

Happily, as far as England is concerned, our law no longer lends its power to enforce such a position.

5.—"*Free human soul* . . ."

Woman's deep and wholesome impulse and yearning for individual freedom and selfdom is well-spoken in the following lines, by an anonymous writer; touchingly shown also is the unsufficingness to her soul of even the most honeyed of unequal positions :—

> "Oh, to be alone !
> To escape from the work, the play,
> The talking every day ;
> To escape from all I have done,
> And all that remains to do.
> To escape—yes, even from you,
> My only love, and be
> Alone and free.
>
> Could I only stand
> Between gray moor and gray sky,
> Where the winds and the plovers cry,
> And no man is at hand ;
> And feel the free wind blow
> On my rain-wet face, and know
> I am free—not yours, but my own—
> Free, and alone !
>
> For the soft firelight
> And the home of your heart, my dear,
> They hurt, being always here.
> I want to stand upright,
> And to cool my eyes in the air,
> And to see how my back can bear
> Burdens—to try, to know,
> To learn, to grow !
>
> I am only you !
> I am yours, part of you, your wife !
> And I have no other life.
> I cannot think, cannot do ;
> I cannot breathe, cannot see ;
> There is 'us,' but there is not 'me' :—
> And worst, at your kiss I grow
> Contented so."

7.—"*From woman slave can come but menial race,*"

If the result to the family is such as I have described

what must be the effect on the race? A slow but sure degeneration. And has this not taken place? Is the race now such as you read of it in early times before the Mogul invasion brought the Zenana and child marriage in its train? Where are the Rajputs and the Mahrattas with their manly exercises and their mental vigour? For centuries you have been children of children, and there is no surer way of becoming servants of servants."—Mrs. Pechey Phipson, M.D. ("Address to the Hindoos," p. 9).

Id. . . "If children are to be educated to understand the true principle of patriotism, their mother must be a patriot."—Mary Wollstonecraft (Letter to Talleyrand).

8.—"*The mother free confers her freedom and her grace.*"

"The child follows the blood of the mother; the son of a slave or serf father and a noble woman is noble. 'It is the womb which dyes the child,' they say in their primitive language. . . . 'The woman bears the clan,' say the Wyandot Indians, just as our ancestors said 'The womb dyes the child!'"—Letourneau ("The Evolution of Marriage," Ch. XI., XVII.).

XLI.

1.—"*By her the progress of our future kind.*"

"What may man be? Who can tell? But what may woman be
To have power over man from cradle to corruptible grave?"

—William Blake ("Jerusalem").

Id. "The application of the Pfeiffer bequest, 'for

charitable and educational purposes in favour of women,' has been delayed by legal difficulties, but the Attorney General has now submitted to the Court of Chancery a first list of awards. Details given in the *Journal of Education* show that Girton and Newnham Colleges receive £5,000 each, whilst Bedford College, Somerville Hall, the New Hospital for Women, the Maria Grey Training College, and a number of other institutions benefit by slightly smaller sums. The bequests will doubtless be welcomed by the recipients, for all the institutions included so far are doing useful work with very inadequate means, and it is to be hoped that the generous example of the London merchant and his literary wife will be often followed in the future. Women's education—and girls', too, for that matter—in this country is almost unendowed, and is yet expected to produce results equal to those gained in the richly endowed foundations for boys and men. The interest of the Pfeiffer bequest, however, lies rather in the spirit that prompted it and in the views of progress held by the donors than in the generosity of the gift or the precise manner of its distribution. In a letter explaining his wishes, Mr. Pfeiffer remarks :—

"I have always had and am adhering to the idea of leaving the bulk of my property in England for charitable and educational purposes in favour of women. Theirs is, to my mind, the great influence of the future. Education and culture and responsibility in more than one direction, including that of politics, will gradually fit them for the exercise of every power that could possibly work towards the regeneration of mankind. It is women who have hitherto had the worst of life, but their interest, and with their interest that of humanity, is secured, and I therefore am determined to help them to the best of my ability and means."—*Manchester Guardian*, June 7th, 1892.

"Men are what their mothers made them. You may as well ask a loom which weaves huckaback, why it does not make cashmere, as expect poetry from this engineer, or a chemical discovery from that jobber. Ask the digger in the ditch to explain Newton's laws; the fine organs of his brain have been pinched by overwork and squalid poverty from father to son, for a hundred years. When each comes forth from his mother's womb, the gate of gifts closes behind him. Let him value his hands and feet, he has but one pair. So he has but one future, and that is already predetermined in his lobes, and described in that little fatty face, pig-eye, and squat form."—Emerson (Essay on Fate).

Id "The British *race* cannot afford to dispense with *all* the advantage that may be in embryo in the future female intellect, because men and some women are found who declare that women are intellectually inferior. . . . No amount of prayers and wishes and submitting to God's will are of any avail. You must *use* the organs of the intellect in order, not only to increase their efficiency, but to prevent their going from bad to worse. It might here be noted, that because the British people might choose to be satisfied with atrophy of the intellect lobes in their mothers, it will not at all follow that other nations will do so *also*. If such things as nations exist, there will always be rivalry and competition, and depend upon it those will be first whose mothers generally possess the most efficient intellect lobes. . . . Fortunately we have learnt another great lesson, evolved by Charles Darwin's frontal lobes, and that is, that there is no such thing as a *fixed* and *unalterable* tissue or organism anywhere. All organisms and parts of organisms are *changeable*. Everything—organ and organism—*has* changed in the past, *is* changing in the present, and *will* change in the future in accordance with the conditions that surround it. Women's frontal lobes and grey matter will certainly be no exception to the rule. Emancipation, keeping her eyes open, and thinking for herself are the three main things she has to keep hammering at, until the lords of creation *see* that they are the right things to do, to save future generations from universal imbecility."—E. Bonavia, M.D. ("Woman's Frontal Lobes").

2.—"*Their stalwart body and their spacious mind.*"

"If she be small, slight-natured, miserable,
How shall men grow?"
—Tennyson ("The Princess," Canto 7).

XLIII.

8.—"*Where lies her richest gift,*

"As I have already said more than once, I consider it presumption in anyone to pretend to decide what women are or are not, can or cannot be by natural constitution. They have always hitherto been kept, as far as regards spontaneous development, in so unnatural a state, that their nature cannot but have been greatly distorted and disguised, and no one can safely pronounce that if women's nature were left to choose its direction as freely as men's, and if no artificial bent were attempted to be given to it except that required by the conditions of human society, and given to both sexes alike, there would be any material difference, or perhaps any difference at all, in the character and capacities which would unfold themselves."—J. S. Mill ("The Subjection of Women," p. 104).

XLIV.

4.— . . . *the freeman, equable*

"The freeman assuredly scorns equally to insult and to be insulted."—Alexander Walker ("Woman as to Mind," p. 205).

XLV.

2.—" . *equal freedom, equal fate* . "

"As long as boys and girls run about in the dirt, and trundle hoops together, they are both precisely alike. If you catch up one half of these creatures and train them to a particular set of actions and opinions, and the other half to a perfectly opposite set, of course their understandings will differ, as one or the other sort of occupations has called this or that talent into action. There is surely no occasion to go into any deeper or more abstruse reasoning in order to explain so very simple a phenomenon."—Sydney Smith ("Female Education").

Id. "Was it Mary Somerville who had to hide her books, and study her mathematics by stealth after all the family had gone to sleep, for fear of being scolded and worried because she allowed her intellect full scope? She has now a bust in the Royal Institution! Whatever view of the case theoretical considerations may suggest, there is one fact beyond cavil, and it is this: that the female frontal lobes are not only capable of equalling in power the male lobes, but can surpass them *when allowed* free scope. This has been recently proved in one of the universities, where a woman surpassed the senior wrangler in mathematics—an essentially intellectual work."—Dr. Emanuel Bonavia ("Woman's Frontal Lobes").

The "girl graduate" last referred to is Miss Philippa Fawcett at the University Examinations, Cambridge, in June, 1890.

3.—"*Together reared* . . ."

"We find a good example in the United States, where, to the horror of learned and unlearned pedants of both sexes, numerous colleges exist in which large numbers of young men and women are educated together. And with what results? President White, of the University of Michigan, expresses himself thus: 'For some years past a young woman has been the best scholar of the Greek language among 1,300 students; the best student in mathematics in one of the classes of our institution is a young woman, and many of the best scholars in natural and general science are also young women.' Dr. Fairchild, President of Oberlin College in Ohio, in which over 1,000 students of both sexes study in mixed classes, says: 'During an experience of eight years as Professor of the ancient languages, Latin, Greek, and Hebrew, and in the branches of ethics and philosophy, and during an experience of eleven years in theoretical and applied mathematics, the only difference which I have observed between the sexes was in the manner of their rhetoric.' Edward H. Machill, President of Swarthmore College, in Pennsylvania, tells us that an experience of four years has forced him to the conclusion that the education of both sexes in common leads to the best moral results. This may be mentioned in passing as a reply to those who imagine such an education must endanger morality."—Bebel ("Women," Walther's Translation, p. 131). (See also Notes to line 7, forward.)

It is of good omen that the precedent thus set in America is finding a following in our own isle also. All honour to the University of St. Andrews, concerning which sundry newspapers of 15th March, 1892, relate that: "The Senatus Academicus of the University of St. Andrews has agreed to open its classes in arts, science, and theology to women, who will be taught along with men. The University will receive next year a sum of over £30,000 to be spent on bursaries, one half of the sum to be devoted to women exclusively. Steps are being taken to secure a hall of residence in which the women students may live while attending the University classes."

Id.—" . . . *in purity and truth,*
Through plastic childhood and retentive youth."

"Je voudrais que ce petit volume apportât au lecteur un peu de la jouissance que j'ai goûtée en le composant. Il complète mes *Souvenirs*, et mes souvenirs sont une partie essentielle de mon œuvre. Qu'ils augmentent ou qu'ils diminuent mon autorité philosophique, ils expliquent, ils montrent l'origine de mes jugements, vrais ou faux. Ma mère, avec laquelle j'ai été si pauvre, à côté de laquelle j'ai travaillé des heures, n'interrompant mon travail que pour lui dire : 'Maman, êtes-vous contente de moi ?' mes petites amies d'enfance qui m'enchantaient par leur gentillesse discrète, ma sœur Henriette, si haute, si pure, qui, à vingt ans, m'entraîna dans la voie de la raison et me tendit la main pour franchir un passage difficile, ont embaumé le commencement de ma vie d'un arome qui durera jusqu'à la mort."—Ernest Renan ("Souvenirs d'Enfance.").

5.—"*Their mutual sports of sinew and of brain*"

"No boy nor girl should leave school without possessing a grasp of the general character of science, and without having been disciplined more or less in the methods of all sciences; so that when turned into the world to make their own way, they shall be prepared to face scientific problems, not by knowing at once the conditions of every problem, or by being able at once to solve it, but by being familiar with the general current of scientific thought, and by being able to apply the methods of science in the proper way, when they have acquainted themselves with the conditions of the special problem."—T. H. Huxley ("Essay on Scientific Education").

And the same learned professor tells us, on another occasion :—"A liberal education is an artificial education which has not only prepared a man to escape the great evils of disobedience to natural laws, but has trained him to appreciate and to seize upon the rewards which Nature scatters with as free a hand as her penalties. That man, I think," (shall we not include "woman" also, on his own showing as above?) "has had a liberal education who has been so trained in youth that his body is the ready servant of his will, and does with ease and pleasure all the work that, as a mechanism, it is capable of; whose intellect is a clear, cold logic engine, with all its parts in equal strength and in smooth working order, ready, like a steam engine, to be turned to every kind of work, and spin the gossamers as well as forge the anchors of the mind; whose mind is stored with a knowledge of the great and fundamental truths of Nature, and of the laws of her operations; one who, no stunted ascetic, is full of life and fire, but whose passions are trained to come to heel by a vigorous will, the servant of a tender conscience; who has learned to love all beauty, whether of Nature or of art, to hate all vileness, and to respect others as himself.

"Such an one, and no other, I conceive, has had a liberal education, for he is as completely as a man can be in harmony with Nature. He will make the best of her, and she of him. They will get on together rarely; she as his ever beneficent mother, he as her mouthpiece, her conscious self, her minister, and interpreter."—*Id.* ("Essay on a Liberal Education.")

6.—"*In strength alike the sturdy comrades train;* . . ."

How largely strength is simply a matter of training may be instanced by a case or two:—

"The results of practice and training from childhood on the bodily development can be seen in female acrobats and circus riders, who could compete with any man in courage, daring, dexterity, and strength, and whose performances are frequently astonishing."—Bebel ("Woman," p. 126).

"I am a medical man. I have spent several years in Africa, and have seen human nature among tribes whose habits are utterly unlike those of Europe. I had been accustomed to believe that the *muscular* system of women is necessarily feebler than that of men, and perhaps I might have dogmatised to that effect; but, to my astonishment, I found the African women to be as strong as our men. . . . Not only did I see the proof of it in their work and in the weights which they lifted, but on examining their arms I found them large and hard beyond all my previous experience. On the contrary, I saw the men of these tribes to be weak, their muscles small and flabby. Both facts are accounted for by the habits of the people. The men are lazy in the extreme; all the hard work is done by the women."—(*Westminster Review*, Oct., 1865, p. 355.)

"Les femmes Sphakiotes ne le cédent en rien aux hommes pour la vigueur et l'energie. J'ai vu un jour une femme ayant un enfant dans les bras et un sac de farine sur la tête, gravir, malgré ce double fardeau, la pente escarpée qui conduit à Selia."—Jules Ballot ("Histoire de l'Insurrection Crétoise," Paris, 1868, p. 251).

Id. . . . In this context it is pleasant to find in the newspapers such a note as the following:—

"The frost continued throughout West Cheshire yesterday, and skating on rather rough ice was largely enjoyed. At Eaton, where the Duke of Westminster is entertaining a party, the guests had a hockey match on the frozen fish-pond in front of the hall. The players, who kept the game up with spirit for over an hour, included the Duchess of Westminster, the Marquis and Marchioness of Ormonde, Lady Beatrice and

Lady Constance Buller, Lord Arthur Grosvenor, Lord Gerald Grosvenor, Lady Margaret and Lady Mary Grosvenor, Captain and Mrs. Cawley, Hon. Mrs. Norman Grosvenor, Hon. Mrs. Thomas Grosvenor, General Julian Hall, and party."—(*Manchester Courier*, 12th Jan., 1892.)

Later on in the year we read in the journal *Woman*:—

"At the Marlow Regatta an extremely pretty girl in navy serge, built Eton fashion, was a Miss ——, who wore as an under-bodice a full vest of shaded yellow Indian silk. Her prowess with the oar is the cause of daily admiration to the Marlowites."

Again, on August 15th, 1892, the *Manchester Evening Mail* has the following:—

"An ailing 'navvy,' who has been engaged in some works near Versailles, was a few days ago admitted to a hospital in that town. Before the sick person had long been in the institution it was discovered that the apparent 'navvy' was a woman. The superintendent of the hospital was not in the least surprised on hearing of the transformation scene, for it appears that he is accustomed to deal with many woman patients who enter the hospital in male attire. It is common in the district (says a Paris correspondent) for robust women to don men's garb in order to obtain remunerative employment as navvies, porters, farm labourers, road menders, or assistants to bricklayers, masons, and builders. It has long been established that the average Frenchwoman of town or country has as great a capacity for work either in counting-houses, shops, fields, or farms as her lord and master has for laziness and lolling in the cafés, playing dominoes, and smoking cigarettes."

On the preceding day, August 14th, 1892, the St. Petersburg journals reported that:—

"Ces jours-ci sera érigé à Sébastopol le monument élevé en l'honneur des Femmes de cette ville qui, en 1854, ont construit seules une batterie contre les troupes alliées. C'est une pyramide taillée en granit d'une hauteur de cinquante pieds.

Sur un côté est écrit en lettres d'or: 'C'est ici que se trouvait la batterie des Femmes'; sur l'autre face les mots suivants sont gravés: 'A cet endroit, en 1854, les Femmes de Sébastopol ont construit une batterie.' Le jour de l'inauguration de ce monument n'est pas encore fixé. L'impératrice se fera représenter à l'inauguration par un grand-duc."

And, in October, 1892, the "sporting" newspapers recorded that:—

"Women are gradually coming to the fore as bicycle riders. Miss Dudley, a well-known rider, has just accomplished a feat which would have seemed wonderful for any rider not long ago. She has ridden from a spot near Hitchin to Lincoln, a distance of 100 miles, in little more than seven hours, or at the average speed of about fourteen miles an hour. Mr. and Mrs. Smith are well known as tandem riders, and they have won many races together; but this is, perhaps, the first recorded instance of a woman cyclist holding her own so well, unaided, in a long road ride."

See also "The Lancashire pit-brow women," Note XVIII., 8.

7.—"*Of differing sex no thought inept intrudes;*"

"I have conversed, as man with man, with medical men on anatomical subjects, and compared the proportions of the human body with artists—yet such modesty did I meet with that I was never reminded by word or look of my sex, and the absurd rules which make modesty a pharisaical cloak of weakness."—Mary Wollstonecraft ("The Rights of Woman," p. 278).

"As a careful observer remarks, true modesty lies in the entire absence of thought upon the subject. Among medical students and artists the nude causes no extraordinary emotion; indeed, Flaxman asserted that the students in entering the Academy seemed to hang up their passions along with their hats."—Westermarck (" History of Human Marriage," p. 194).

Id. . "This is strikingly exemplified in the curious conversation recorded in Lylie's 'Euphues' and his 'England,' edit. 1605, 4to, signature X—Z 2, where young unmarried people of both sexes meet together and discuss without reserve the ticklish metaphysics of love. But though treading on such slippery ground, it is remarkable that they never, even by allusion, fall into grossness. Their delicate propriety is not improbably the effect of their liberty."—Buckle ("Common-place Book," No. 856).

8.—" *Their purpose calmly sure all errant aim excludes.*"

" We point to a present remedy for undergraduate excesses, which, resting on the soundest theory, has also the demonstration of unquestioned fact. It is co-education. Cease to separate human beings because of sex. They are conjoined in the family, in the primary and grammar schools, in society, and, after the degree rewards four years of monastic student existence, in the whole career of life.

"Throw open the doors of Harvard to women on equal terms, absorb the annexe into the college proper, and as the night follows the day, scholarship will rise and dissipation fall by the law of gravitation. The moral atmosphere will find immediate purification, and the daily association of brothers and sisters in intellectual pursuits impart a breadth of view which is an education in itself. The professors may then be left safely to their themes, John Harvard's statue may cease to dread defilement, the regent will find his censorial duties fully as perfunctory as he seems to have made them in the past, and character will crowd out profligacy."—William Lloyd Garrison (in *Woman's Journal*, Boston, U.S., 6th February, 1892).

"Whatsoever is ultimately decided by the wisdom of ages to be the best possible form of culture for one human nature, must be so for another, for one common humanity lies deeper in all and is more essential in each than any difference."—Sophia Jex-Blake, M.D.

XLVI.

3.— . . . *impartial range*

Preparation in this direction is going steadily forward, not only in the Western hemisphere, but in the Eastern. It is announced (in August, 1892) that

"Lady students at the five Universities in Switzerland number 224. Berne is the most popular, with 78 female undergraduates; Zurich has 70; Geneva 70; the new University of Lausanne has five; and Basle one. The medical faculty is in most favour with the female students, and counts 157 of the whole number; the philosophical faculty follows with 62; five prefer the faculty of jurisprudence; the theological faculty has not yet been invaded by the sex. More than half of the female students, 116, are Russians, 21 Germans, 21 Swiss, 11 Americans,, nine Austrians, seven Bulgarians, four English, three Roumanians, and three from the Turkish Empire, all of whom are young Armenian ladies."

4.— . . . *wider wisdom*

Such wider wisdom—without the preliminary suffering—as the poet had attained to, when he wrote :—

"I have climbed to the snows of Age, and I gaze at a field
in the Past,
Where I sank with the body at times in the sloughs
of a low desire;
But I hear no yelps of the beast, and the man is quiet
at last,
As he stands on the heights of his life with a glimpse
of a height that is higher."

—Tennyson ("By an Evolutionist").

Id.—" . . . *juster ethics, teach;* . . ."

"For we see that it is possible to interpret the ideals of ethical progress, through love and sociality, co-operation and sacrifice, not as mere utopias contradicted by experience, but as the highest expressions of the central evolutionary process of the natural world. . . . The older biologists have been primarily anatomists, analysing and comparing the form of the organism, separate and dead; however incompletely, we have sought rather to be physiologists, studying and interpreting the highest and intensest activity of things living. . . . It is much for our pure natural history to recognise that 'creation's final law' is not struggle, but love."—Geddes and Thomson ("The Evolution of Sex," pp. 312, 313).

5, 6.—"*Conformed to claims of intellect and need,*
The tempered numbers of their highborn breed;"

"There is a problem creeping gradually forward upon us, a problem that will have to be solved in time, and that is the steady increase of population. . . . I believe that with the emancipation of women we shall solve this problem now. Fewer children will be born, and those that are born will be of a higher and better physique than the present order of men. The ghastly abortions, which in many parts pass muster nowadays, owing to the unnatural physical conditions of society, as men, women, and children, will make room for a nobler and higher order of beings, who will come to look upon the production of mankind in a diseased or degraded state as a wickedness and unpardonable crime, against which all men and women should fight and strive."—Lady Florence Dixie ("Gloriana," p. 137).

Id. . . And Mrs. Mona Caird says:—"If the new movement had no other effect than to rouse women to rebellion against the madness of large families, it would confer a priceless benefit on humanity."—(*Nineteenth Century*, May, 1892.)

Id. "To bring a child into existence without a fair prospect of being able, not only to provide food for its body, but instruction and training for its mind, is a moral crime, both against the unfortunate offspring and against society. . . . The fact itself of causing the existence of a human being, is one of the most responsible actions in the range of human life. To undertake this responsibility—to bestow a life which may be either a curse or a blessing—unless the being on whom it is bestowed will have at least the ordinary chances of a desirable existence, is a crime against that being. And in a country either overpeopled, or threatened with being so, to produce children, beyond a very small number, with the effect of reducing the reward of labour by their competition, is a serious offence against all who live by the remuneration of their labour."—J. S. Mill ("Liberty," Chap. V.).

Id. . . A. Dumas fils draws a true and piteous picture in which this element of the unintelligent over-production of human beings has the largest share :—

"Il y a, et c'est la masse, les femmes du peuple et de la campagne suant du matin au soir pour gagner le pain quotidien, faisant ainsi ce que faisaient leurs mères, et mettant au monde, *sans savoir pourquoi* ni comment, des filles qui, à leur tour, feront comme elles, à moins que, plus jolies, et par conséquent plus insoumises, elles ne sortent du groupe par le chemin tentant et facile de la prostitution, mais où le labeur est encore plus rude. Le dos courbé sous le travail du jour, regardant la terre quand elles marchent, domptées par la misère, vaincues par l'habitude, asservies aux besoins des autres, ces créatures à forme de femme ne supposent que leur condition puisse être modifiée jamais. Elles n'ont pas le temps, elles n'ont jamais eu la faculté de penser et de réfléchir ; à peine un souhait vague et bientôt refoulé de quelque chose de mieux ! Quand la charge est trop lourde elles tombent, elles geignent comme des animaux terrassés, elles versent de grosses larmes à l'idée de laisser leurs petits sans ressources, ou elles remercient instinctivement la mort, c'est à dire le repos dont elles ont tant besoin." ("Les Femmes qui Tuent," etc., p. 101.)

Id. And again, the advanced biological writers say :—

"The statistician will doubtless long continue his fashion of confidently estimating the importance and predicting the survival of populations from their quantity and rate of reproduction alone; but at all this, as naturalists, we can only scoff. Even the most conventional exponent of the struggle for existence among us knows, with the barbarian conquerors of old, that 'the thicker the grass, the easier it is mown,' that 'the wolf cares not how many the sheep may be.' It is the most individuated type that prevails in spite, nay, in another sense, positively because of its slower increase; in a word, the survival of a species or family depends not primarily upon quantity, but upon quality. The future is not to the most numerous population, but to the most individuated. . . .

"Apart from the pressure of population, it is time to be learning (1) That the annual childbearing still so common, is cruelly exhaustive to the maternal life, and this often in actual duration as well as quality; (2) That it is similarly injurious to the standard of offspring; and hence, (3) That an interval of two clear years between births (some gynæcologists even go as far as three) is due alike to mother and offspring." (It is to be noted that this period of three years is postulated as a necessity for the well-being of the offspring; it is by no means a recommendation to even a triennial maternity on the part of the mother, who is indeed to be, in all fulness, "free mistress of her person's sacred plan," with a duty to herself, as well as to her child). "It is time, therefore, as we heard a brave parson tell his flock lately, 'to have done with that blasphemous whining which constantly tries to look at a motherless' (ay, or sometimes even fatherless) 'crowd of puny infants as a dispensation of mysterious providence.' Let us frankly face the biological facts, and admit that such cases usually illustrate only the extreme organic nemesis of intemperance and improvidence, and these of a kind far more reprehensible than those actions to which common custom applies the names, since they are species-regarding vices, and not merely self-regarding ones, as the others at least primarily are. . . .

"It seems to us, however, essential to recognise that the ideal to be sought after is not merely a controlled rate of increase, but regulated married lives. . . . We would urge, in fact, the necessity of an ethical rather than of a mechanical 'prudence after marriage,' of a temperance recognised to be as binding on husband and wife as chastity on the unmarried. . . . Just as we would protest against the dictum of false physicians who preach indulgence rather than restraint, so we must protest against regarding artificial means of preventing fertilisation as adequate solutions of sexual responsibility. After all, the solution is primarily one of temperance. It is no new nor unattainable ideal to retain, throughout married life, a large measure of that self-control which must always form the organic basis of the enthusiasm and idealism of lovers."—Geddes and Thomson ("The Evolution of Sex," Chap. XX.).

As a fitting exemplification of the words of the "parson" above narrated, compare the following verbatim extract from a conversation in this year of grace 1892. The —— referred to is a man about 35, middle-class, and of "good 'education'" (!) The same description would also apply to the speaker, who said, "Poor —— is a brave fellow, and keeps up his head in the worst of luck. He has a lot of home troubles; he has lost three children, and his wife always has a bad time at the birth of each baby."

No word of sympathy for the wife and mother, or even of recognition that it was really *she* who bore the pain at each "bad time." As the children left alive still numbered two at the time of the speech, the whole incident can but imply—on the part of both actor and speaker—the hideous, even if unconscious, inhumanity so widely prevalent. Never will "high-born breed" be attained till such action of low-bred intellect is reprobated and amended; in accordance with the enunciated truth, that:—

"Especially in higher organisms, a distinction must obviously be drawn between the period at which it is possible for males and females to unite in fertile sexual union, and the period at which such union will naturally occur or will result in the fittest offspring."—Geddes and Thomson (*op. cit.*, p. 243).

7, 8. "*Not overworn with childward pain and care,*
The mother—and the race--robuster health shall share."

"It is not the true purpose of any intellectual organism to live solely to give birth to succeeding organisms; its duty is also to live for its own happiness and well-being. Indeed, in so doing, it will be acting in one of the most certain ways to ensure that faculty and possession of happiness that it aims to secure for its progeny."—Ben Elmy ("Studies in Materialism," Chap. III.).

Id. . . . Even the placid and precisian American poet bears strong, if involuntary, testimony to the evil and wrong of the non-cultured and untempered begetting of children:—

"She wedded a man unlearned and poor,
And many children played round her door;
But care and sorrow, and child-birth pain
Left their traces on heart and brain."
—Whittier ("Maud Müller").

Id. Mr. Andrew Lang also promises us "a world that is glad and clean, and not overthronged and not overdriven."—(Introduction to "Elizabethan Songs.")

Id. . . "Justice never loses sight of *self.* The language of Justice is 'to Me and to You; or to You and to Me.' . . . We have to learn, for the action and spirit worthy of the coming time, that woman is never to sacrifice herself to a man, but, when needful, to the *Manhood* she hopes or desires to develop in him. In this she will also attain her own development. But after the hour when her faith in the hope of worthy results fails her (reason instructing her nobler affections by holding candidly in view all the premises, past, present, and future), she is bound by all her higher obligations to bring that career, whether it be of the daughter, sister, mother, wife, or friend, to a close. For the inferior cannot possibly be worth the sacrifice of the superior. True self-sacrifice, which necessarily involves the temporary descent of the nobler to the less noble—the higher to the lower—is made only when the lower is elevated, improved, carried forward in its career, thereby."—Eliza W. Farnham ("Woman and Her Era," Vol. II., p. 149).

Id. "I have urged on woman independence of man, not that I do not think the sexes mutually needed by one another; but because in woman this fact has led to an excessive devotion which has cooled love, degraded marriage, and prevented either sex from being what it should be to itself or the other. . . . Woman, self-controlled, would never be absorbed by any relations; it would be only an experience to her as to man. It is a vulgar error that love, *a* love to woman, is her whole existence; she is also born for truth and love in their universal energy."—Margaret Fuller Ossoli ("The Woman of the Nineteenth Century").

Id. . . Professor Alfred Russell Wallace has written an article, concerning part of which Mr. W. T. Stead rightly says: "It is a scientific reinforcement of the cause of the emancipation of women, and shows that progress of the cause of female enfranchisement is identified with the progress of humanity."—(*Review of Reviews*, Vol. V., p. 177.)

Professor Wallace says:—

"When such social changes have been effected that no woman will be compelled, either by hunger, isolation, or social compulsion, to sell herself, whether in or out of wedlock, and when all women alike shall feel the refining influence of a true humanising education, of beautiful and elevating surroundings, and of a public opinion which shall be founded on the highest aspirations of their age and country, the result will be a form of human selection which will bring about a continuous advance in the average status of the race. Under such conditions, all who are deformed either in body or mind, though they may be able to lead happy and contented lives, will, as a rule, leave no children to inherit their deformity. Even now we find many women who never marry because they have never found the man of their ideal. When no woman will be compelled to marry for a bare living or for a comfortable home, those who remain unmarried from their own free choice will certainly increase, while many others, having no inducement to an early marriage, will wait till they meet with a partner who is really congenial to them.

"In such a reformed society the vicious man, the man of degraded taste or feeble intellect, will have little chance of finding a wife, and his bad qualities will die out with himself. The most perfect and beautiful in body and mind will, on the other hand, be most sought, and, therefore, be most likely to marry early, the less highly endowed later, and the least gifted in any way the latest of all, and this will be the case with both sexes.

"From this varying age of marriage, as Mr. Galton has shown, there will result a more rapid increase of the former than of the latter, and this cause continuing at work for successive generations will, at length, bring the average man to be the equal of those who are now among the more advanced of the race."—"Human Progress, Past and Present" (*Arena*, Jan., 1892).

XLVII.

1.—"*Nor blankly epicene* . . "

"Bring up a boy and girl side by side, and educate them both for the same profession under the same masters, and a novelist who depicts character could yet weave a story out of the mental and emotional differences between them, which will cause them to look at life from totally opposite points of view."—Mabel Collins ("On Woman's Relation to the State").

2.—" . *sequence of that day.*"

"We have seen that a deep difference in constitution expresses itself in the distinctions between male and female, whether these be physical or mental. The differences may be exaggerated or lessened, but to obliterate them it would be necessary to have all the evolution over again on a new basis. What was decided among the Prehistoric Protozoa cannot be annulled by Act of Parliament."—Geddes and Thomson (" Evolution of Sex," p. 267).

3, 4.—" *not . . . by aping falser sex shall truer grow.*"

" While man and woman still are incomplete
I prize that soul where man and woman meet,
Which types all Nature's male and female plan,
But, friend, man-woman is not woman-man."

—Tennyson (" On One who Affected an Effeminate Manner ").

XLVIII.

8.—" *Happy what each may bring to help the common fate.*"

" I would submit to a severe discipline, and to go without many things cheerfully, for the good and happiness of the human race in the future. Each one of us should do something, however small, towards that great end. . . . How pleasant it would be each day to think, to-day I have done something that will tend to render future generations more happy. The very thought would make this hour sweeter. It is absolutely necessary that something of this kind should be discovered. . . . It should be the sacred and sworn duty of everyone, once at least during lifetime, to do something in person towards this end. It would be a delight and a pleasure to me to do some thing every day, were it ever so minute. To reflect that another human being, if at a distance of ten thousand years from the year 1883, would enjoy one hour's more life, in the sense of fulness of life, in consequence of anything I had done in my little span, would be to me a peace of soul."—Richard Jefferies ("The Story of My Heart," pp. 129, 131, 160).

XLIX.

1.—"*By mutual aid perfecting complex man.*"

Kant says: "Man and woman constitute, when united, the whole and entire being, one sex completes the other."—Bebel ("Woman," Walther's Translation, p. 44).

2, 3.—"*Their two-fold vision human life may scan*
From differing standpoints "

See Note XLVII., 1.

LI.

4.—"*Her brain untutored*

"The soldier is exercised in the use of his weapons, the artisan in the use of his tools. Every profession demands a special education, even the monk has his novitiate. Women alone are not prepared for their important maternal duties."—Irma von Troll-Borostyani ("Die Mission unseres Jahrhunderts." A Study on the Woman Question).

LIII.

2.— . . . *the quivering nerve*

"M. Chauveau states that his object was 'To ascertain

the excitability of the spinal marrow, and the convulsions and pain produced by that excitability.' His studies were made chiefly on horses and asses, who, he says, 'lend themselves marvellously thereto by the large volume of their spinal marrow.' M. Chauveau accordingly 'consecrated eighty subjects to his purpose.' 'The animal,' he says, 'is fixed upon a table. An incision is made on its back about fourteen inches long; the vertebræ are opened with the help of a chisel, mallet, and pincers, and the spinal marrow is exposed." (No mention is made of anæsthetics, which of course would nullify the experimenter's object of studying "the excitability of the spinal marrow, and the convulsions *and pain* produced by that excitability.") "M. Chauveau gives a large number of his cases. . . . Case 7: 'A vigorous mule. When one pricks the marrow near the line of emergence of the sensitive nerves, the animal manifests the most violent pain.' Case 20: 'An old white horse, lying on the litter, unable to rise, but nevertheless very sensitive. At whatever points I scratch the posterior cord I provoke signs of the most violent suffering.'"—(*Journal de Physiologie*, du Dr. Brown-Séquard. Tome Quatrième. No. XIII.)

4.—" . . *living butchery with learned knife.*"

"We are told what Professor Brücke says with reference to section of the trigeminus:—'The first sign that the trigeminus is divided is a loud piercing cry from the animal. Rabbits we know,' he adds, 'are not very sensitive; all sorts of things may be done to them without making them utter a cry; but in this operation, if it succeeds, they invariably send forth a prolonged shriek.'"—"Lectures on Physiology," Vol. II., p. 76.

5.—" *cruel anodyne that chained the will*

It is dubious whether curare be even an anodyne, *i.e.* a deadener of pain. M. Claude Bernard, himself a vivisector, says:—"Curare acting on the nervous system only suppresses the action of the motor nerves, leaving sensation intact. Curare is not an anæsthetic." (*Revue Scientifique*, 1871-2, p. 892.)

6.—" . . . *the shuddering victim conscious still.*"

"Everyone has heard of the dog, suffering under vivisection, who licked the hand of the operator; this man, unless he had a heart of stone, must have felt remorse to the last hour of his life."—Darwin ("The Descent of Man," Part I., Chap. II.).

8.—"*Nor yields her holiest truths on such a murderer's rack.*"

"It is fit to say here, once for all, that laws which govern the animal kingdom below the human, can no more be accepted as final and determining to man, in physiological, than in intellectual and moral, action. For neither the knife of the anatomist, nor the lens of the microscopist, are infallible interpreters of function. We do not possess ourselves of all of Nature's secrets by cutting up her tissues and fabrics, neither by the keenest inspection of their ultimate atoms, whether fluid or solid. There are some truths withheld from the investigator, however brave, patient, and nice his methods and means, which are given up, in due time, to the truth-seer, without any method or means, save the intuitive faculty and its unambitious, guileless surrender to the service offered it. Such, it is at least possible, we may find has been Nature's dealing in this occult department."—Eliza W. Farnham ("Woman and Her Era," Vol. I., pp. 47, 50).

LIV.

1.—"*True science finds its own by kindlier quest.*"

"Science is of the utmost importance to mankind, but the last degree of importance cannot be said to attach to all its minute discoveries, and where, as in physiology, the investigation becomes inhuman, there it ought to stop. It ought to stop for our own sakes if from no other motive, for the torturing of animals on the chance that it may suggest the means of alleviating some of our own pains helps to blunt those sensibilities which afford us some of our purest pleasures. Animals are not our equals in all things, but they seem to be at any rate our equals in the sense of pain. The want of imagination may deprive it in their case of some of its poignancy, but on the other hand they have none of the supports which we derive from reason and sympathy, from the tenderness of friendship and the consolations of religion. With them it is pure, unmitigated, unsolaced suffering. Our duties to them form a neglected chapter in the code of ethics, but we ought not to torture them, and there are many who will maintain that the obligation is absolute. Life is no doubt valuable, but it is not everything. It is more than meat, as the body is more than raiment, but it is not more than humanity. There are occasions on which it has to be risked, and there are terms on which men of honour and patriotism would hold it worthless. The doctrine that we may subject the lower animals to incredible suffering on the possibility that it may save ourselves from an additional pang is of a selfish and degrading tendency. It helps to lower the 'moral ideal' and to weaken the springs of heroism in human character. We owe it to ourselves to keep clear of this peril. Nature surrounds us with limitations. Here is one which all that is best and noblest in us sets up, and it is more sacred than those over which we have no control. We refuse to torture other sentient creatures in order that we may live."—Dr. Henry Dunckley (*Manchester Guardian*, August 9th, 1892).

The above noble pronouncement, with its conclusion, is instinct with the spirit of *true* science (which repudiates with disdain and horror the hypocritical pseudo-science of a ghastly and demoralising study and pursuit of cruelty),—the *true* science which is one with love, because it refuses the acceptance of life itself on terms of outrage to love.

See Note LXI., 3.

4.— . . . *a keener lens of man's own brain.*"

"Observation is perhaps more powerful an organon than either experiment or empiricism."—Richard Jefferies ("Story of My Heart," p. 162).

Id. . . It is well that some English physicists of the fullest scientific impulse and effort are revolted at the inhuman and bootless cruelty of the foreign medical schools which masquerades as scientific research. Is it not possibly something more than a coincidence that vivisectionists in general exhibit an aversion to the equality of woman, and that vivisection flourishes more unrestrainedly where her position and influence are less recognised; *i.e.*, in plain words,—in a lower civilisation?

Mr. Lawson Tait says, with the indignation of a truly scientific mind at these methods of "science falsely so called":—

"For one, as intimately and widely concerned in the application of human knowledge for the saving of human life and the relief of human suffering as anyone can be, or as anyone has ever been, I say I am grateful for the restrictive legislation. Let me give one brief illustration of my most recent experience in this matter as one of hundreds which confirm me in my determination persistently to oppose the introduction into England of what passes for science in Germany. Some few years ago I began to deal with one of the most dreadful calamities to which humanity is subject by means of an operation which had been scientifically proposed nearly two hundred years ago. I mean ectopic gestation. The *rationale* of the proposed operation was fully explained about fifty years ago, but the whole physiology of the normal process and the pathology of the perverted one were obscured and misrepresented by a French physiologist's experiments on rabbits and dogs. Nothing was done, and at least ninety-five per cent. of the victims of this catastrophe were allowed to die.

"I went outside the experimentalists' conclusions, went back to the true science of the old pathologist and of the surgeon of 1701, and performed the operation in scores of cases with almost uniform success. My example was immediately followed throughout the world, and during the last five or six years hundreds if not thousands of women's lives have been saved, whilst for nearly forty years the simple road to this gigantic success was closed by the folly of a vivisector.

"Views such as mine are those of a minority of my professional brethren, and are generally sneered at as those of a crank. But my reply to this is that they form the new belief, that of the coming generation, and that not one in fifty of the bulk of my present brethren have ever seriously gone into the question, and probably have never seen a single experiment on a living animal.

"My address as the Surgical Orator of 1890, when the British Medical Association met in this town, was mainly directed to the mischievous system of so-called scientific training, of purely German origin and thoroughly repugnant to our English tastes and our English common sense.

"It is therefore a satisfactory matter to know that the Council of Mason's College would have none of it, and that the governing body of the new University College of Nottingham has recently decided similarly. The Medical School of Queen's College is now united entirely with the Science School of Mason's College; but we, of Mason's College, have had the direction of the science teaching of the Medical School for several years, we have had no German scientific methods, and our success has not diminished thereby one atom—on the contrary."—Lawson Tait, F.R.C.S., *President of Mason's Science College, Birmingham* ("The Discussion on Vivisection at the Church Congress, October, 1892").

At the Congress, as above, Professor Horsley made aspersions on Miss Frances Power Cobbe, as to statements concerning Vivisection in her work, "The Nine Circles." The professor declared some of the reported cruel experiments to have been painless, owing to the victims being under the influence of anæsthetics. In reply to the attack, the following preliminary letter from Miss Cobbe was then published:—

"TO THE EDITOR OF THE 'TIMES.'

"SIR,—Professor Horsley's criticism on the above work—planned and compiled by my direction—demands from me a careful reply, which I shall endeavour to give as soon as may be possible at this distance from the books whence the impugned passages are derived. I shall be much surprised if the hocus pocus of the sham anæsthetic *curare* with ineffective applications of genuine chloroform do not once more illustrate 'the curse of vivisectible animals,' and if the results of the experiments in question, whatever were their worth, would not, in most cases, have been vitiated had real and absolute anæsthesia been produced in the victims. Should a small number of the experiments cited in the 'Nine Circles' prove, however, to have been performed on animals in an entirely painless state, I shall, while withdrawing them with apologies from a forthcoming new edition of the book, take care at the same time to call attention to the multitude of other experiments, home and foreign, therein recorded—*e.g.*, baking to death, poisoning, starving, creating all manner of diseases, inoculating in the eyes, dissecting out and irritating the exposed nerves, causing the brain of cats 'to run like cream,' etc., about which no room for doubt as to the unassuaged agony of the animal can possibly exist."

Miss Cobbe concludes by a sharp, but just, criticism on her critic, and with an acute diagnosis of the learned vivisectionist's own condition :—

"The tone of Dr. Horsley's remarks against me personally will probably inspire those who know me and the history of my connexion with the anti-vivisection cause with an amused sense of the difficulty wherein the Professor must have found himself when, instead of argument in defence of vivisection, he thus turned to 'abuse the plaintiffs' attorney.' For myself I gladly accept such abuse (or mere bluster) as evidence that the consciences even of eminent vivisectors are, like their victims' nerves, imperfectly under the influence of the scientific anæsthesia, and remain still sensitive to the heart-pricking charge which I bring against them, of cowardly cruelty to defenceless creatures.

"I am, Sir, yours,

"FRANCES POWER COBBE.

"Hengwrt, Dolgelly, Oct. 8th, 1892."

⁂ A further newspaper correspondence concerning "The Nine Circles," a work from which some of the foregoing notes on vivisection are copied, has gone on while

"Woman Free" is passing through the press; the vivisectors saying that certain of the incidents transcribed in "The Nine Circles" are without the announcement that in some cases an anæsthetic had been administered prior to the act of living anatomy, otherwise admittedly true in every detail. The vivisectors lay what stress they can on the omissions; indeed, their principal advocate has made use of a grossness of imputation and a coarseness of invective that augurs ill for any gentleness of treatment or purpose being existent in the organism of such an operator.

Yet, in truth, it is not a matter of surpassing import whether the assertion of the operation (alone) being conducted under an anæsthetic be indubitable, since the after-consequences of pain or incommodity had to be endured by the victim without anæsthetics. What initial chloroforming could ward off the constant after-suffering attendant on the incubation of the disease for the creation of which the "operation" had been performed, a period acknowledgedly often lasting for weeks, and terminated only by death's mercy? Or what medicament could anæsthetise the impotent yearning—to feed her starving puppy—of a poor mother dog whose mammary glands had been excised, even if the "operation" had been carried out "under chloroform"? Mr. Edward Berdoe, M.R.C.S., reproduces and reprobates the incident with horror in the *Times* of Oct. 27, 1892:—

"Professor Goltz amputated the breast of the mother of a puppy nursing her young who 'unceasingly licked the living puppy with the same tenderness as an uninjured dog might do.'"

Most gladly may we turn to the words and ways of worthier seekers after truth. Professor Lawson Tait is reported by the *Standard*, 28th Oct., 1892, as saying at a meeting the previous day:—

"Vivisection was a survival from mediæval times. It could not be justified by any results that it had produced. In days when they could tell the composition of the atmosphere of Orion by means of the spectroscope, it was a disgrace that men should resort to vivisection, instead of perfecting other and more humane means of research."

There speaks true science. And, on a later occasion, Mr. Lawson Tait quotes the celebrated anatomist, Sir Charles Bell (who had been falsely claimed as an advocate of vivisection), as saying, "on page 217 of the second volume of his great work on the Nervous System, published in 1839":—

" . . . . a survey of what has been attempted of late years in physiology will prove that the opening of living animals has done more to perpetuate error than to confirm the just views taken from the study of anatomy and natural motions. . . . For my own part I cannot believe that Providence should intend that the secrets of nature are to be discovered by means of cruelty, and I am sure that those who are guilty of protracted cruelties do not possess minds capable of appreciating the laws of nature."—(The *Times*, Nov. 8th, 1892, p. 3.)

The views of Charles Bell and Lawson Tait are in striking and encouraging coincidence with verses LIII., LIV., and LV.

To women peculiarly it belongs to oppose the doctrines and methods of vivisectionists, for to the practitioners of that school were due the arguments or assumptions which sufficed to introduce for a while into our country the vile system of according a licence to male dissoluteness and female subjection—under a pretext of public morality and "scientific" sanction—known on the continent as the "police des mœurs," and in sundry Naval and Military stations of England and Ireland as the "Contagious Diseases Acts."

LV.

8.— . . . *from Love's might alone all thoughts of Wisdom grow."*

"Hast thou considered how the beginning of all thought worthy the name is love; and the wise head never yet was, without first the generous heart?"—Carlyle ("French Revolution," Vol. III., p. 375).

LVI.

5.—" *With woman honoured, rises man to height."*

"If a Hindoo principality is strongly, vigilantly, and economically governed; if order is preserved without oppression, if cultivation is extended, and the people prosperous, in three cases out of four that principality is under a woman's rule. This fact, to me an entirely unexpected one, I have collected from a long official knowledge of Hindoo Governments."—J. S. Mill ("The Subjection of Women," p. 100 note).

6.—" *With her degraded, sinks again in night."*

"And you who have departed from the common tradition, how have you fared in the race of life? Are your men as brave and fearlessly truthful, are your women as courageous and honest as in the old days of 'the maiden's choice'? Are the little worn-out child-wives of to-day likely to have descendants like those of the damsels of your ancient epics? Where are the deeds of high emprise, of daring valour, and of patient persistence of the youths who were fired by the pure love of a woman? Ah! gentlemen, with love life departs; there is no vitality in married life without affection, and when love, the great incentive to action, disappears from the family, leaving dry the streams of affection which should flow between the children and parents, what must come of the race?"—Mrs. Pechey Phipson, M.D. ("Address to the Hindoos").

Id. . . "From all we know of the laws of life and its development it would appear one of the foolishest things on earth for men to fancy that they can debase the intellect lobes of women, and at the same time exalt their own. No breeder of cattle or horses would think of debasing the qualities, in the females, which he would desire to possess in the males.

"No race in the future can either rule the world or even continue in existence without improving the intellect of that race, and this certainly cannot be done by depauperising the intellects of more than half of the *progenitors* of that race."—Dr. E. Bonavia ("Woman's Frontal Lobes").

8.— . . . *Earth's advancing queen.*"

"Will man den ganzen Menschen studiren, so darf man nur auf das weibliche Geschlecht seine Augen richten: denn wo die Kraft schwacher ist, da ist das Werkzeug um so künstlicher. Daher hat die Natur in das weibliche Geschlecht eine naturliche Anlage zur Kunst gelegt. *Der Mann ist geschaffen, ueber die Natur zu gebieten, das Weib aber, den Mann zu regieren.* Zum Ersten gehört viel Kraft, zum Andern viel Geschicklichkeit."—Immanuel Kant.

LVII.

1.—" . *in jealousy*

The male conceit and jealousy of sex, existent among the majority of meaner men, has been perceived and censured or satirised by higher masculine minds both in ancient and modern literature. To take a few scattered instances from the latter, Shakspeare says :—

> " . . . however we do praise ourselves,
> Our fancies are more giddy and infirm,
> More longing, wavering, sooner lost and won
> Than women's are."
>
> —("Twelfth Night," Act II., Sc. 4.)

Goethe says pungently (in "Wilhelm Meister's Apprenticeship"): "People ridicule learned women and dislike even women who are well informed, probably because it is considered impolite to put so many ignorant men to shame."

As our own plain-spoken Sydney Smith has said, in his essay on Female Education :—"It is natural that men who are ignorant themselves, should view, with some degree of jealousy and alarm, any proposal for improving the education of women."

A ludicrously pitiful modern-day instance of the jealous ignorance or ignorant jealousy to which Goethe and Sydney

Smith make reference, is afforded by a seriously-written leading article in No. 545 of the *Christian Commonwealth*, a London weekly newspaper, under date of 24th March, 1892:—

"The Woman question will not down. She is asserting herself in every direction, and generally with considerable force. In America she is positively alarming the lords of creation by her rapid progress in educational matters. She is actually outrunning the men in the race for intellectual attainments. And this fact is becoming so evident, and so prominent, that a new problem is being evolved from it. This is, how are the finely educated young women of America to find congenial husbands? It is assumed by some writers that already there is a great disparity between the culture of the young men and young women, and that every year the chasm between them is becoming deeper and wider. This is a truly lamentable state of things, but the woman movement in this country is likely to take a more practical course. The agitation of the question of Woman Suffrage may bring about a reaction against her excessive culture. If woman is permitted to enter the cesspool of politics, it is probable she will not be very long distressed with an overplus of those qualities which are just now endangering her conjugal felicity in the United States. . . ."

It is refreshing and consolatory to revert from such verbiage to what Sir Humphrey Davy said ("Lectures, 1810 and 1811"): "It has been too much the custom to endeavour to attach ridicule to the literary and scientific acquisitions of women. Let *them* make it disgraceful for men to be ignorant, and ignorance will perish."

To Shakspeare and Goethe may be added the corroboration of French intellect:—

"Nest-il pas évident que Molière, dans ses *Femmes Savantes* n'a pas attaqué l'instruction, l'étude, mais le pédantisme, comme, dans son *Tartuffe*, il avait attaqué non la vraie dévotion, mais l'hypocrisie? N'est-ce pas Molière lui-même qui a écrit ce beau vers: "Et je veux qu'une femme ait des clartés *de tout?*"—Monseigneur Dupanloup, Evêque d'Orléans ("Femmes Savantes et Femmes Studieuses," 1868, p. 8).

"C'est à Condorcet et non pas à Jean Jacques, comme on le croit généralement, qu'appartient l'initiative des réformes proposées dans l'éducation et la condition des femmes."—Daniel Stern ("Hist. de la Révolution de 1848," Vol. II, p. 185).

"Quand la loi française"—(shall we not say also every other?)—"déclare la femme inférieure à l'homme ce n'est jamais pour libérer la femme d'un devoir vis-à-vis de l'homme ou de la societé, c'est pour armer l'homme ou la societé d'un droit de plus contre elle. Il n'est jamais venu à l'idée de la loi de tenir compte de la faiblesse de la femme dans les différents délits qu'elle peut commettre; au contraire, la loi en abuse."—A. Dumas fils ("Les Femmes qui Tuent," etc., p. 204).

Mill says:—"There is nothing which men so easily learn as this self-worship; all privileged persons, and all privileged classes have had it." And he also speaks of a time—"when satires on women were in vogue, and men thought it a clever thing to insult women for being what men made them."—("Subjection of Women," pp. 76, 77).

We have seen (Note XLV., 5) how Professor Huxley postulates scientific training equally for girls and boys; he has also said:—"Emancipate girls. Recognise the fact that they share the senses, perceptions, feelings, reasoning powers, emotions of boys, and that the mind of the average girl is less different from that of the average boy, than the mind of one boy is from that of another; so that whatever argument justifies a given education for all boys, justifies its application to girls as well."—("Emancipation, *Black and White.*")

Balzac asserted: "A woman who has received a masculine education possesses the most brilliant and fertile qualities, with which to secure the happiness of her husband and herself."—("Physiologie du Mariage," Méditation XI.).

But the instances are innumerable where the intellect of higher men expressly or unconsciously rebukes the jealous sexual conceit of their less intelligent brethren. Dr. Bonavia says, very tersely:—"The fact is, many men don't like the idea of being surpassed or even equalled by women. They stupidly feel their dignity wounded. This jealousy, however, is not only extremely contemptible and unjust, but disastrous to the true interests of the race, for men have mothers *as well as women*, and imbecility—the result of atrophied frontal lobes—is just as likely to be transmitted to the one sex as to the other, as far as we yet know. Just see the injustice of men's jealousy in matters of intellect. Only recently the talent of Miss Ormerod—an entomologist who can hold her own *anywhere* on earth—was kept under by the Royal Agricultural Society. *She* did the entomological work, and made the discoveries, while *they* took the credit. In their reports they did not even mention *her* name in connection with her own work!—A more contemptible proceeding, it would appear, has never been brought to light, in the struggle of the sexes, if that case has been correctly reported."—("Woman's Frontal Lobes.")

Bebel treats this jealousy with a fine irony in his exposition of "the motives which induce most medical professors, and indeed the professors of every faculty, to oppose women students."—"They regard the admission of women as synonymous with the degradation of science (!) which could not but lose its prestige in the eyes of the enlightened (!) multitude if it appeared that the female brain was capable of grasping problems which had hitherto only been revealed to the elect of the opposite sex."—(*Op. cit.*, p. 132.)

Had Bebel recorded masculine mercenary considerations, rather than sham misgivings as to the interests of science, his sarcasm would have been very grim truth. Indeed, what is sometimes called the "loaves and fishes" argument is at the root of most of this masculine jealousy which cloaks itself under a pretension of tender consideration for woman's delicacy. To cite Bebel again: "Another objection is that it is unseemly to admit women to medical lectures, to operations, and deliveries, side by side with male students. If men see nothing indecent in studying and examining female patients in the presence of nurses and other female patients, it is difficult to understand why it should become so through the presence of female students."—(*Op. cit.*, p. 132.) And as to the actual fitness of women for exercising the profession of medicine or surgery:—

"'Women always improve when the men begin to show signs of failing,' were the words of a distinguished physician and surgeon, who had seen years of service on a remote wintry station of the army. 'I have had fellows brought to me to have the leg amputated—perhaps both—close to the body, and never anywhere in Paris, London, or New York, saw I better surgeon's assistants than some of our women made, especially the Sisters of Charity, of whom we had a few at the post, for three or four years. Heads as clear as a silver bell; hands steady and unshrinking as a granite rock, yet with a touch as light as a spring leaf; foot quick and indefatigable, whether the time was noon-day or midnight; memory perfect; tenderness for the sufferer unfailing. Talk about love, courage, fortitude, and endurance in your sex! I tell you,' he added, with a needless affimation at this point, 'they seem to be nothing else, when these are most wanted, and the man who doubts them is an ass'"—Eliza W. Farnham ("Woman and Her Era," Vol. II., p. 157). See also Note XXIX., 8.

Id. Here may fittingly follow the report of a trained masculine judgment as to woman's ability in yet a further profession—that of the law:—

At the recent opening of the Southern California College of Law, at Los Angeles, John W. Mitchell, the president, in his lecture upon "The Study of the Law," spoke of the utility of women studying law, in the following language:—

"This part of this discourse it is believed would be radically incomplete without calling attention to one other and particular class of persons who need an insight into the rudiments of law—which class, it seems, has also been neglected by those occupying a like position to my own—I mean the women. He is, indeed, blind to the signs of the times who does not recognise the expanding field of women's work, and their increased influence in the professions as well as in the fine arts.

That women are entering the lists with men, in behalf of themselves and womankind, is well; for they must make up their minds to take up the task of urging the reforms they need, and must solve the woman problem in all its bearings. Women are doing this. They are becoming competitors with men in the pursuits of life, it is true; but it is as much from necessity as choice. But it is not only the women who have to labour and earn their own living who need legal knowledge to aid them. It is more needful to the woman of property, be her possessions but an humble home or a colossal fortune; whether she be married or single. Women want this experience to make them cautious of jeopardising their rights, and less confiding in business matters. The courts are full of cases showing how women have been wrongly stripped of their belongings. And, perhaps, if one woman had known the legal effect of some of her acts, one of the largest fortunes ever amassed in this State of Crœsus-like wealth would not have been carried to distant States, and there scandalously distributed amongst scheming adventurers and lawyers, making a little Massachusetts county-seat the theatre of one of the most remarkable contests for a fortune in the whole annals of probate court law.

"As to the professions: women were for a long time barred from them, but now the barriers to all of them have been removed, and there is not a profession in which women are not distinguished. They have graduated in the sciences from most universities with the highest honours, and have stood the same tests as the men. The law was about the last to admit them within its precincts, and there they are meeting with an unexpected measure of success. Not only in this, but in other countries, there are successful women practitioners. And in France, where the preparatory course is most arduous, and the term of study longest, a woman recently took the highest rank over 500 men in her graduating examinations, and during the whole six years of class study she only lost one day from her work—an example that is commended to you students. Undoubtedly, the weight of the argument is in favour of women studying law."—(*Women's Journal*, Boston, U.S., 6th February, 1892.)

Id. . . Even the vaunted politeness and gallantry of the Frenchman is not proof against the far more deeply-bedded masculine jealousy. M. de Blowitz, the erudite correspondent at Paris of the *Times*, reports that—

"The law students yesterday hooted down Mdlle. Jeanne Chauvin, 28 years of age, who was to have argued a thesis for a legal degree. She had chosen as her theme, 'The Professions accessible to Women and the Historical Evolution of the Economic Position of Woman in Society.' The uproar was such that the examiner postponed the ceremony *sine die.* Mdlle. Chauvin is the first Frenchwoman who has sought a legal degree, but two years ago a Roumanian lady went through the ordeal without obstruction."—(The *Times*, July 4, 1892.)

To revert to the "loaves and fishes" argument, an incident now to be given will show that medicine and the law are not the only professions in which the objections to the equal status of the sexes are largely prompted by a "jalousie de métier" of a selfish and mercenary character :—

"The following letters have been received at Auckland from the Vice-Chancellor of the University of Cambridge in relation to the memorial lately sent from New Zealand in favour of the opening of degrees to women :—

"'Dear Professor Aldis,

"'Your very interesting memorial reached me yesterday. I still await the explanatory letter and analysis. After receiving I will write again.

"'Yours etc.,
"'John Peile,
"'Vice-Chancellor.

"'Christ's College Lodge,
"'Cambridge, Nov. 2nd, 1891.'

"'My Dear Professor Aldis,

"'The petition of the memorial received by me from Miss Lilian Edger and yourself, respecting degrees for women at the University of Cambridge, and the analysis of the signatures to that memorial, have been printed by me in the *University Reporter*, the official organ of communication of any kind of business to the members of the Senate. The memorial itself will be preserved in the Registry of the University. Immediate action on this question by the Council of the Senate—the body, with which, as you are aware, all legislation in the University must begin—is not probable. The question was raised about three years ago; and it became at once plain that, if persevered in, it would produce a very serious division in the ranks of those members of the University who had all shown themselves, in the past, friends to the highest education of women. Many of those who had earnestly supported the admission of women to Tripos examinations, *would not support their admission to the B.A. degree.* Into their—mostly practical—reasons I cannot fully enter: One was the belief that admission to B.A. must lead, in the end (in spite of any provisions which might be introduced), to admission to M.A., and consequently to *a share in the management of the University;* it was also apprehended that difficulties would arise in the several colleges *with respect to fellowships, etc.* I do not mention these difficulties as insuperable. But they are felt by so many that there is, I am persuaded, no prospect of successful action in this matter at the present time. I shall, therefore, not myself propose anything in the Council, nor so far has any other of the friends of women's education, of whom there are many on the Council, given notice of any motion. At any future time, when such a motion is made, your most influential memorial will certainly have its due weight with the members of the Council, and if they decide to take action, I hope also, with members of the Senate.

"'I am, etc.,

"'JOHN PEILE,

"'Vice-Chancellor of the University of Cambridge.

"'Christ's College Lodge,

"'Cambridge, Nov. 20th, 1891.'"

—(*New Zealand Herald*, 5th Jan., 1892.)

6.—" . . . *potency* . . "

"The Brain is different from all other organs of the body. It is often a mass of structural potentialities rather than of fully-developed nerve tissues. Some of its elements, viz., those concerned with best-established instinctive operations, naturally go on to their full development without the aid of extrinsic stimuli; others, however, and large tracts of these, seem to progress to such developments only under the influence of suitable stimuli. Hence natural aptitudes and potencies of the most subtle order may never be manifested by multitudes of persons, for want of the proper stimuli and practice capable of perfecting the development and functional activity of those regions of the brain whose action is inseparably related to the mental phenomena in question."—Dr. H. C. Bastian ("The Brain as an Organ of Mind," p. 374).

LVIII.

1.—"*Woman's own soul must seek and find*

On women of medical education especially is the duty incumbent to investigate the world of biological experience in woman. They may not sit quietly down and assume that in learning all that man has to teach, they rest his equals, and that the last word has been said on the matter. They have a field of exploration, with opportunities, with implements, and with capacities, which man cannot have. His research on such a question as the recognisedly most vital one of human embryology with all its issues, can get but rare and uncertain light from accidental occasions, and is, moreover, simply as it were a dead anatomising; nor can he by any means reach the psychic or introspective phase of enquiry; but woman has the live subject, body and soul, in her own organism, to study at her leisure. Does she not yet see how to grasp such further living knowledge? But that is the very quest here indicated. The askidian also had no strength of vision, yet we can now tell and test the light and the components of distant spheres.

There are, undoubtedly, what may be termed intelligent operations carried on in the body unconsciously to oneself, or at any rate beyond the present ken of one's actively perceptive and volitional faculties. Observation and recognition of these is to be striven for, and even guidance or command of them may be ours in a worthy future. The *Times* of 27th January, 1892, reported a lecture at the Royal Institution on the previous day by Professor Victor Horsley, in the course of which the lecturer—

> " . pointed out the pineal gland, which Descartes thought to be the seat of the soul, but which was now known to be an invertebrate eye. He also explained the functions of certain small masses of grey matter, which are two, viz.—sight and equilibration. The optic nerve was situated close to the crura, and equilibration was subserved by the cerebellum. After referring to the basal ganglia, Professor Horsley admitted that as science advanced we seem to know less and less about the specific functions of the various masses of grey matter, and less definite views than formerly prevailed were now held with respect to the local source of what are termed voluntary impulses, and that of sensations. . We were still in ignorance as to the functions of the optic thalamus, and of the corpus striatum. Those of the cortex had to some extent been ascertained. They might be divided into three classes, viz.—movement, sensation, and what was termed mental phenomena. But we were still in the dark as to those portions of the brain which subserved intellectual operations, memory, and emotional impulses. A like ignorance prevailed with respect to the basal ganglia."

What as yet unrecognised inward eyes watch over the embryo life?

3.—' . . . *counsel helpful* .

Mrs. Eliza W. Farnham says:—"In this day the most needed science to humankind is that which will commend women to confidence in themselves and their sex as the leading force of the coming Era—the Era of spiritual rule and movement; in which, through them, the race is destined to rise to a more exhalted position than ever before it has held, and for the first time to form its dominant ties of relationship to that world of purer action and diviner motion, which lies above the material one of intellectual struggle and selfish purpose wherein man has held and exercised his long sovereignty."—("Woman and Her Era," Vol. I., p. 311).

5.—" . . . *philosophic lore* . . "

"The farther our knowledge advances, the greater will be the need of rising to transcendental views of the physical world. If the imagination had been more cultivated, if there had been a closer union between the spirit of poetry and the spirit of science, natural philosophy would have made greater progress because natural philosophers would have taken a higher and more successful aim, and would have enlisted on their side a wider range of human sympathies."—Buckle ("Influence of Women on the Progress of Knowledge").

Id. . . . *chirurgic lore* . "

"The Lady Dufferin fund had already been the means of

opening a school of medicine for Indian women, who would consequently devote themselves to the study of anatomy. Anatomy and Asiatic women. That was the most extraordinary association of ideas one could ever have imagined." —Professor Vambéry (Lecture to the Royal Scottish Geographical Society, Edinburgh, 20th May, 1891). Reported in the *Times* of following day.

8.—"*Regent of Nature's will,* . ."

"Woman will grow into fitness for the sublime work which nature has given her to do, and man through her help and persuasion will spontaneously assume the relation of a co-operator in it. Finding that nature intends his highest good and that of his species, through the emancipation and development of woman into the fulness of her powers, he will gratefully seek his own profit and happiness in harmonising himself with this method; he will honour it as nature's method, and woman as its chief executor; and will joyfully find that not only individuals, families, and communities, but nations, have been wisely dependent on her, in their more advanced conditions, for the good which can come only from the most perfect, artistic, and spiritual being who inhabits our earth."—Eliza W. Farnham ("Woman and Her Era," Vol. II., p. 423).

LIX.

1.—"*Each sequent life shall feel her finer care.*"

"The one thing constant, the one peak that rises above all clouds, the one window in which the light for ever burns, the one star that darkness cannot quench, is *woman's love.* This one fact justifies the existence and the perpetuation of the human race. Again I say that women are better than men; their hearts are more unreservedly given; in the web of their lives sorrow is inextricably woven with the greatest joys; self-sacrifice is a part of their nature, and at the behest of love and maternity they walk willingly and joyously down to the very gates of death. Is there nothing in this to excite the admiration, the adoration, of a modern reformer? Are the monk and nun superior to the father and mother?"—Robert Ingersoll (*North American Review*, Sept., 1890).

2.—"*Each heir of life a wealthier bounty share;*"

Poets and physiologists agree in these prognostications. The keen observer, Bastian, in his treatise on archebiosis, willingly calls to his support an equally conscientious ally, in the following passage:—

"We must battle on along the path of knowledge and of duty, trusting in that natural progress towards a far distant future for the human race, such as its past history may warrant us in anticipating. For, as Mr. Wallace points out, those natural influences which have hitherto promoted man's progress 'still acting on his mental organisation, must ever lead to the more perfect adaptation of man's higher faculties to the conditions of surrounding nature and to the exigencies of the social state,' so that 'his mental constitution may continue to advance and improve, till the world is again inhabited by a single, nearly homogeneous race, no individual of which will be inferior to the noblest specimens of existing humanity.'"—Dr. H Charlton Bastian ("The Beginnings of Life," Vol. II. p. 633).

3.—" *Those lives allied in equal union chaste* "

"The great chastity of paternity, to match the great chastity of maternity."

—Walt Whitman ("Children of Adam").

4.—" *A sweeter purpose, purer rapture, taste;*"

"A wife is no longer the husband's property; and, according to modern ideas, marriage is, or should be, a contract on the footing of perfect equality between the sexes. The history of human marriage is the history of a relation in which women have been gradually triumphing over the passions, the prejudices, and the selfish interests of men."—Edward Westermarck (Concluding words of "The History of Human Marriage").

7.—" *The only rivalry* . . . . . .

"When woman finds her proper place in legislation, it will be found ultimately that it will be not as man's rival, but his helpmate."—Mabel Collins ("On Woman's Relation to the State").

8.—" *How for their lineage fair still larger fate to find.*"

"Lycurgus, the Spartan lawgiver, had the idea of making public principle and utility predominate over private interests and affections; and on that idea he ordained that children were not to be the property of their parents, but of the State, which was to direct their education, and determine their modes of life. A better idea with the legislators of the future—*the number of whom will be equal with that of all wholesomely-developed men and women upon the earth*—will be to take fullest advantage of all natural instincts. The parents, their hearts ever yearning with love for their offspring, and the community, careful of its individual members, co-operating in placing the children under all good influences towards that development, which, being the best for their individual lives, will also coincide with what is best for the general welfare. For this end, the experience of the past, and the higher wisdom of their own times, will far better qualify them to judge of fitting means and methods than we can now either surmise or suggest."—David Maxwell ("Stepping-stones to Socialism," p. 15).

LX.

1.—"*Their task ineffable yields wondrous gain.*"

"I rest not from my great task;
To open the eternal worlds! To open the immortal eyes
Of man inwards; into the worlds of thought: into eternity
Ever expanding the human imagination."

—William Blake ("Jerusalem").

2.—"*Their energies celestial force attain.*"

"Les écrivains du dix-huitième siècle ont sans doute rendu d'immenses services aux Sociétés; mais leur philosophie basée sur le sensualisme, n'est pas allée plus loin que l'épiderme humain. Ils n'ont considéré que l'univers extérieur, et, sous ce rapport seulement, ils ont retardé, pour quelque temps, le développement morale de l'homme. . . . L'étude des mystères de la pensée, la découverte des organes de l'AME humaine, la géometrie de ses forces, les phénomènes de sa puissance, l'appréciation de la faculté qu'elle nous semble posséder de se mouvoir indépendamment du corps, de se transporter où elle veut et de voir sans le secours des organes corporels, enfin les lois de sa dynamique et celles de son influence physique, constitueront la glorieuse part du siècle suivant dans le trésor des sciences humaines. Et nous ne sommes occupés peutêtre, en ce moment, qu' à extraire les blocs énormes qui serviront plus tard à quelque puissant génie pour bâtir quelque glorieux édifice."—Balzac ("Physiologie du Mariage," Méditation XXVI.).

3, 4.—"*Their intermingled souls, with passion dight,*
In aspiration soar past earthly height."

"As yet we are in the infancy of our knowledge. What we have done is but a speck compared to what remains to be done. For what is there that we really know? We are too apt to speak as if we had penetrated into the sanctuary of truth and raised the veil of the goddess, when, in fact, we are still standing, coward-like, trembling before the vestibule, and not daring, from very fear, to cross the threshold of the temple. The highest of our so-called laws of nature are as yet purely empirical.

" They who discourse to you of the laws of nature as if those laws were binding upon nature, or as if they formed a part of nature, deceive both you and themselves. The (so-called) laws of nature have their sole seat, origin, and function in the human mind. They are simply the conditions under which the regularity of nature is recognised. They explain the external world, but they reside in the internal. As yet we know scarcely anything of the laws of mind, and, therefore, we scarcely know anything of the laws of nature. We talk of the law of gravitation, and yet we know not what gravitation is; we talk of the conservation of force and distribution of forces, and we know not what forces are; we talk with complacent ignorance of the atomic arrangements of matter, and we neither know what atoms are nor what matter is; we do not even know if matter, in the ordinary sense of the word, can be said to exist; we have as yet only broken the first ground, we have but touched the crust and surface of things. Before us and around us there is an immense and untrodden field, whose limits the eye vainly strives to define; so completely are they lost in the dim and shadowy outline of the future. In that field, which we and our posterity have yet to traverse, I firmly believe that the imagination will effect quite as much as the understanding. Our poetry will have to reinforce our logic, and we must feel as much as we argue. Let us then hope, that the imaginative and emotional minds of one sex will continue to accelerate the great progress, by acting upon and improving the colder and harder minds of the other sex."—Buckle (" Influence of Women on the Progress of Knowledge ").

6.—" . *the vision to retain,*"

As with Wordsworth's nature-nurtured maiden :—

> " . . . beauty born of murmuring sound
> Shall pass into her face . . .
> And vital feelings of delight
> Shall rear her form to stately height .
> The floating clouds their state shall lend
> To her ; for her the willow bend,
> Nor shall she fail to see
> Even in the motions of the storm
> Grace that shall mould the maiden's form
> By silent sympathy."
>
> —(" Poems of the Imagination ").

Id. " My hope becomes as broad as the horizon afar, reiterated by every leaf, sung on every bough, reflected in the gleam of every flower. There is so much for us yet to come, so much to be gathered, and enjoyed. Not for you or me, now, but for our race, who will ultimately use this magical secret for their happiness. Earth holds secrets enough to give them the life of the fabled Immortals. My heart is fixed firm and stable in the belief that ultimately the sunshine and the summer, the flowers and the azure sky, shall become, as it were, interwoven into man's existence. He shall take from all their beauty and enjoy their glory. He is indeed despicable who cannot look onwards to the ideal life of man. Not to do so is to deny our birthright of mind."—R. Jefferies (" The Pageant of Summer ").

7, 8.—" . . . *mould their dreams of love, with conscious skill*
To human living types

"Her Brain enlabyrinths the whole heaven of her bosom and loins
To put in act what her Heart wills."
—William Blake ("Jerusalem").

"These states belong so purely to the inner nature; are so deeply hidden beneath the strata of what we call the inner life, even, that only women, and of these only such as have become self-acquainted, through seeing the depths within the depths of their own consciousness, can fully comprehend all that is meant in the words a 'Purposed Maternity.' I use them in their highest sense, meaning not the mere purpose of satisfying the maternal instincts, which the quadruped feels and acts from, as well as the human being, but the intelligent, artistic purpose (to which the maternal instinct is a fundamental motive), to act in harmony with Nature in producing the most perfect being which the powers and resources employed, can bring forth. . . . It is probable that we shall, ere long, arrive at truer views of maternity everywhere; and when we do, I think it will be seen that the office has a sacredness in Nature's eyes above all other offices, and that she reserves for it the finest of her vital forces, powers, susceptibilities, and means of every sort."—Eliza W. Farnham ("Woman and Her Era," Vol. II., p. 385; Vol. I., p. 93).

[It has been an intense delight to come upon these and the other words and thoughts of Eliza W. Farnham;

"blazes" or axe-marks of this previous pioneer in the same exploration. It is only since completing the whole of the verses that the writer has found the passages quoted from Mrs. Farnham's work, and deduces a not unnatural confirmation of the mutually shared views, from the singular concord and unanimity of their expression.]

8.—" . . . *supreme of form and will.*"

"The changes that have come over us in our social life during the past two decades are, in many respects, remarkable, but in no particular are they so remarkable as in the physical training and education of women. . . .

"The results of this social change have been on the whole beneficial beyond expectation. The health of women generally is improving under the change; there is amongst women generally less bloodlessness, less of what the old fiction-writers called swooning; less of lassitude, less of nervousness, less of hysteria, and much less of that general debility to which, for want of a better term, the words '*malaise*' and 'languor' have been applied Woman, in a word, is stronger than she was in olden time. With this increase of strength woman has gained in development of body and of limb. She has become less distortioned. The curved back, the pigeon-shaped chest, the disproportioned limb, the narrow feeble trunk, the small and often distorted eyeball, the myopic eye, and puny ill-shaped external ear—all these parts are becoming of better and more natural *contour*. The muscles are also becoming more equally and more fully developed, and with these improvements, there are growing up amongst women models who may, in due time, vie with the best models that old Greek culture has left for us to study in its undying art."—Dr. Richardson ("The Young Woman," Oct., 1892).

Id.—" . . . prophetic scenes,
Spiritual projections
In one, the sacred parturition scene,
A happy, painless mother births a perfect child."
—Walt Whitman ("Autumn Rivulets").

Id. . . "I am so rapt in the beauty of the human form, and so earnestly, so inexpressibly prayerful to see that form perfect, that my full thought is not to be written. . . . It is absolutely incontrovertible that the ideal shape of the human being is attainable to the exclusion of deformities. When the ambition of the multitude is fixed on the ideal form and beauty, then that ideal will become immediately possible, and a marked advance towards it could be made in three generations."—Richard Jefferies ("The Story of My Heart," pp. 32, 151, 131).

Id.

"'The Gods?' In yourselves will ye see them, when Venus shall favour your love,
And man, fitly mated with woman, believes that his love is divine:
When passion shall elevate woman to something so holy and grand
That she—the ideal enraptured—shall ne'er be a check upon Man,
Then the children they bear will be holy, and beauty shall make them her own,

And man in the eyes of his neighbour will gaze on the reflex divine
Of the God he inclines to in spirit—or trace in each feature and limb
The lines which the body inherits from souls which are noble and true.

Would thou couldst feel in deep earnest, how beautiful God will be then,
When we see Him as Jove or Apollo in men who inspire us with love,
As Juno and Venus the holy, in women who know not the mean,
And feel not the influence cruel of hardness and self-love and scorn.
Would thou couldst once know how real the presence of God will become,
How earnest and ever more earnest thy faith when thyself shall be great,
And from the true worship of others thoult learn what is holy in them,
And rise to the infinite fountain of glory which flows in us all."

—C. G. Leland ("The Return of the Gods").

LXI.

3.—" *Their science*

" Science then
Shall be a precious visitant; and then
And only then, be worthy of her name:

For then her heart shall kindle; her dull eye,
Dull and inanimate, no more shall hang
Chained to its object in brute slavery;
But taught with patient industry to watch
The processes of things, and serve the cause
Of order and distinctness, not for this
Shall it forget that its most noble use,
Its most illustrious province, must be found
In furnishing clear guidance, a support
Not treacherous, to the mind's *excursive* power."
—Wordsworth ("The Excursion," Book IV.).

4.—" . . . *crude dimensions* . . ."

"In these material things, too, I think that we require another circle of ideas, and I believe that such ideas are possible, and, in a manner of speaking, exist. Let me exhort everyone to do their utmost to think outside and beyond our present circle of ideas. For every idea gained is a hundred years of slavery remitted. Even with the idea of organisation, which promises most, I am not satisfied, but endeavour to get beyond and outside it, so that the time now necessary may be shortened."—Richard Jefferies ("Story of My Heart," p. 180).

8.—"*The love that lifts the life from rank of earth to heaven.*"

" . . . utter knowledge is but utter love—
Æonian Evolution, swift and slow,
Thro' all the spheres—an ever opening height,
An ever lessening earth."
—Tennyson ("The Ring").

Id.

"The light of love
Not failing, perseverance from their steps
Departing not, they shall at length obtain
The glorious habit by which sense is made
Subservient still to moral purposes,
Auxiliar to divine. That change shall clothe
The naked spirit, ceasing to deplore
The burthen of existence
—— So build we up the Being that we are;
Thus deeply drinking-in the soul of things,
We shall be wise perforce; and, while inspired
By choice, and conscious that the Will is free,
Unswerving shall we move as if impelled
By strict necessity, along the path
Of order and of good. Whate'er we see,
Whate'er we feel, by agency direct
Or indirect, shall tend to feed and nurse
Our faculties, shall fix in calmer seats
Of moral strength, and raise to loftier heights
Of love divine, our intellectual soul."
—Wordsworth ("The Excursion," Book IV.).

LXII.

1, 2.—" . . . *wingèd words on which the soul would pierce*
Into the height of love's rare Universe."

The two lines are Shelley's, in his "Epipsychidion."

7.—"*Man's destiny with woman's blended be.*

". . . . in the long years liker must they grow;
The man be more of woman, she of man."
—Tennyson ("The Princess," Part VII.).

Id.—"Dans ma manière de sentir, je suis femme aux trois quarts."
—Ernest Renan ("Souvenirs d'Enfance").

Id.

"Das Ewigweibliche
Zieht uns hinan."
—Goethe (concluding two lines of "Faust").

8.— . . . *progression,* . . .

"Unfolded out of the folds of the woman, man comes unfolded, and is always to come unfolded;
Unfolded only out of the superbest woman of the earth, is to come the superbest man of the earth;
Unfolded out of the friendliest woman is to come the friendliest man;
Unfolded only out of the perfect body of a woman can a man be form'd of perfect body;
Unfolded only out of the inimitable poem of the woman, can come the poems of man
Unfolded out of the folds of the woman's brain come all the folds of the man's brain, duly obedient;
Unfolded out of the justice of the woman all justice is unfolded;
Unfolded out of the sympathy of the woman is all sympathy;

A man is a great thing upon the earth, and through eternity—but every jot of the greatness of man is unfolded out of woman,
First the man is shaped in the woman, he can then be shaped in himself."

—Walt Whitman ("Leaves of Grass").

LXIII.

2.— . . . *the dream men named Divine,—"*

"Divine" was the title of honour conferred on the "Commedia," by the repentant citizens of Florence, after the death of Dante.

8.—" *The love that moves the sun and every circling star."*

The last line of the "Divina Commedia" is—

"Lo amor che move il sole e le altre stelle."

EPILOGUE.

What, then, is the result of these investigations?

Briefly this:

That woman is not incapable of equal mental and physical power with man:

That where any inferiority on her part at present exists, it is but as the inherited result of long ages of misuse of her functions, and of want of training of her faculties:

That an intelligent education in both directions can repair these wrongs, and establish her due individuality, and her equal share in human right and happiness:

"That the principle which regulates the existing social relations between the two sexes—the legal subordination of one sex to the other—is wrong in itself and now one of the chief hindrances to human improvement; and that it ought to be replaced by a principle of perfect equality, admitting no power or privilege on the one side, nor disability on the other" (JOHN STUART MILL, "The Subjection of Women," Ch. I.):

And that, as the result of woman's amended position, the whole human race will benefit physically and psychically.

Thus much, at least, may be fairly concluded from the "Notes" here presented; in the gathering together of which scattered rays—thoughts and experiences from many an observant mind—into one focus, to offer light and warmth to suffering womanhood and humanity, the main purpose of this book is accomplished.

E. E.

January 1st, 1893.

*** *The courtesy of corroborations or elucidations (confidential or otherwise) of the subject-matter of these Notes is invited by the Author (care of Mrs. Wolstenholme Elmy, Buxton House, Congleton), with a view to a possible fuller edition.*

INDICES, &c

AUTHORITIES OR REFERENCES IN NOTES

INDEX TO NOTES.

[By the law of England a girl is still marriageable at twelve and a boy at fourteen years of age; though the "age of consent" to intercourse not thus sanctioned has been recently raised to sixteen years in the case of girls. In the above matters, and notably in that of the marriageable age, England remains barbarously below most modern legislatures, and is indeed in the disgraceful condition of being not even on a level with China, in which country—as Mr. Byrant Barrett points out, in his Introductory Discourse to the "Code Napoléon," p. 66—"In females, it would appear, consummation is not allowable before twelve," while "the age for marriage in males is twenty complete." China and England are but slightly in advance of ancient India, where, according to the precepts of Manu, as Mr. Barrett further shows, (p. 30), "The male of 24 years should marry the girl of 8 years of age; the male of 30 the female of 12" (Ordinances of Manu, ch. 9, sec. 94). Is not such conduct as this sufficient to involve as inevitable consequences "unripe maternity and untimely birth," together with all their dire inherited miseries?]

See also the following:—

"But I hear you indignantly reject the boon of equality with such creatures as men now are. With you I would equally elevate both sexes. Really enlightened women, disdaining equally the submissive tricks of the slave and the caprices of the despot, breathing freely only in the air of the esteem of equals, and of mutual, unbought, uncommanded, affection, would find it difficult to meet with associates worthy of them in men as now formed, full of ignorance and vanity, priding themselves on a *sexual* superiority, entirely independent of any merit, any superior qualities, or pretentions to them, claiming respect from the strength of their arm, and the lordly faculty of producing beards attached by nature to their chins! No: unworthy of, as incapable of appreciating, the delight of the society of such women, are the great majority of the existing race of men. The pleasures of mere animal appetite, the pleasures of commanding (the prettier and more helpless the slave, the greater these pleasures of the brute), are the only pleasures which the majority of men seek from women, are the only pleasures which their education and the hypocritical system of morals, with which they have been necessarily imbued, permit them to expect . To wish for the enjoyment of the higher pleasures of sympathy and communication of knowledge between the sexes, heightened by that mutual grace and glow, that decorum and mutual respect, to which the feeling of perfect, unrestrained equality in the intercourse gives birth, a man must have heard of such pleasures, must be able to conceive them, and must have an organisation from nature or education, or both, capable of receiving delight from them when presented to him. To enjoy these pleasures, to which their other pleasures, a few excepted, are but the play of children or brutes, the bulk of men want a sixth sense; they want the capacity of feeling them, and of believing that such things are in nature to be found. A mole cannot enjoy the "beauties and glories" of the visible world; nor can brute men enjoy the intellectual and sympathetic pleasures of equal intercourse with women, such as some are, such as all might be. Real and comprehensive knowledge, physical and moral, equally and impartially given by education, and by all other means to both sexes, is the key to such higher enjoyments.

Demand with mild but unshrinking firmness, perfect equality with men: demand equal civil and criminal laws, an equal system of morals, and, as indispensable to these, equal political laws, to afford you an equal chance of happiness with men, from the development and exercise of your faculties."

— William Thompson ("Appeal of One Half the Human Race," 1825, pp. xii, 195).

[The impotent and contradictory schemes of ethics which philosophers or schoolmen, ancient and modern, have successively evolved, have been but resultants of "unisexual wit. With brilliant exceptions in Plato, Kant, and Mill, vainly may the various codes be searched for any suggestion of the identity, individuality, and equality, of woman. For though the philosophy of latter-day ethicists rightly disdains to reiterate or to countenance the factitious scriptural dogmas and imprecations declaratory or explanatory of woman's unequal and subjugated condition, yet a parallel subjection and inferiority in her nature is still tacitly assumed, and on occasion traded upon, by these same ethicists; no counsel or consent of her own intelligence being asked, or disavowal recked of, in such propositions as, *e.g.*, the "utilitarian" theses concerning her enounced by Archdeacon Paley or Mr. Jeremy Bentham; — the nominally "goddess," but virtually "slave," status assigned to her by M. Auguste Comte; — or the "due" amount of childbearing postulated as prior to all "normally feminine mental

"One of those who fought to the last on the rebels' side was the Ranee, or Princess, of Jhansi, whose territory had been one of our annexations. For months after the fall of Delhi she contrived to baffle Sir Hugh Rose and the English. She led squadrons in the field. She fought with her own hand. She was engaged against us in the battle for the possession of Gwalior. In the uniform of a cavalry officer she led charge after charge, and she was killed among those who resisted to the last. Her body was found upon the field, scarred with wounds enough in the front to have done credit to any hero. Sir Hugh Rose paid her the well-deserved tribute which a generous conqueror is always glad to be able to offer. He said, in his general order, that 'The best man upon the side of the enemy was the woman found dead, the Ranee of Jhansi.'"—Justin McCarthy ("History of Our Own Times," chap. xiii).

And on the 12th December, 1892, the *Manchester Guardian* reports:—

"The death is announced of Mrs. Eliza E. Cutler, wife of the doorkeeper of the United States Senate. In February, 1863, her husband's regiment was at Fort Donelson and Mrs. Cutler was visiting him there, stopping at a house just outside the fortification. The colours of the regiment were also in this house. In the excitement which followed the first attack on the day of battle, the regiment went into action without its flag, but just as the fighting became the hottest, with odds terribly against them, they were cheered by the appearance of a woman with a sword in one hand, and bearing triumphantly aloft the regiment's colours. This was Mrs. Cutler, who remained on the battlefield until her husband's regiment was ordered on board a transport in the Cumberland river. She immediately went to the upper